FRENCH RIVER

CANOEING THE RIVER OF THE STICK-WAVERS

FRENCH RIVER

CANOEING THE RIVER OF THE STICK-WAVERS

TONI HARTING

THE BOSTON MILLS PRESS

Canadian Cataloguing in Publication Data
Harting, Toni,
French River : canoeing the river of the stick-wavers
ISBN 1-55046-163-X
1. Canoes and canoeing - Ontario - French River (Parry Sound).
2. French River (Parry Sound, Ont. : River). I. Title.
GV776.15.F74H3 1996   797.1'22'0971315   C96-930151-0

Design by Mary Firth
Printed in Canada

The publisher gratefully acknowledges the support of the Canada Council, and the Ontario Arts Council,
in the development of writing and publishing in Canada.

First published in 1996 by
The Boston Mills Press
132 Main Street
Erin, Ontario, Canada
N0B 1T0
519-833-2407   fax 519-833-2195

An affiliate of Stoddart Publishing Co. Ltd.
34 Lesmill Road
North York, Ontario, Canada
M3B 2T6

Chi-miigwech nwii wiinmowaag kina endaawaad, miinwaa ebiyaawaad enso niibiing oma
Wemitigoozhi Ziibiing. Niibwa ngii wiidookaagook, tibaajmowaad aan gaa bizhiwebak gyet maa
ziibiing gwaag.

Ce livre est affectueusement dédié aux résidents permanents et saisonniers de la région de la
Rivière des Français, dont bon nombre, m'ayant gracieusement ouvert leurs foyers et leurs coeurs,
m'ont aussi apporté le secours des intimes connaissances qu'ils ont sur leur rivière bien-aimée.

I affectionately dedicate this book to all permanent and seasonal residents of the French River
area, many of whom graciously opened their homes and hearts to me while providing important
insights into their beloved river.

And to Ria, of course.

Petite Faucille (Little Sickle) in the Old Voyageur Channel, Western Outlets, looking east.

Contents

Looking north in the Georgian Bay arm south of the Pickerel River Outlet.

PREFACE

This book is the offspring of a passionate love affair.

It all started in the spring of 1985 when I was visiting the French River for the first time in the company of my wife, Ria, and some friends from the Wilderness Canoe Association. While we were camping on an island and enjoying the fabulous waves of Blue Chute, I felt the first stirrings of a very special feeling that over the years and through many visits blossomed into a stimulating relationship I have not had with any of the other rivers I have paddled over the years.

Because I yearned to learn as much as possible about this new love of mine, I began to collect information on the river's natural history and its fascinating past. I not only wanted to experience the entire river and its surrounding country, I also needed to understand the role the French River had played in the fur trade with the colorful coureurs de bois, the voyageurs, Champlain, Mackenzie, and countless others who had paddled its waters in their search for fame and fortune. Above all I longed to find out how and where these people of the past had travelled on this river, to see in my mind's eye the fur traders traversing the same portages as I, facing the same rapids and canoe-crushing rocks I had encountered in my adventures.

But I soon found out that in the late 1980s only a small number of modern publications presented useful information about the French River (especially about the fur-trade times). The few journals written by early travellers make captivating reading, but those have rarely been quoted in the context of the French River itself.

The information coming out of Eric Morse's pioneering work was most useful because of the new insights it offered into these formative years of Canadian history. His publications on the routes of the fur trade are revered classics that instilled in me a strong desire to investigate the French River and its fascinating past in considerable detail.

None of the studies I read, however, provided an overview of the relevant material on the river's topography and history. So, while exploring a favorite area in the Western Outlets during the summer of 1989, I made an important decision. If I really wanted the river and its historical relevance to be known and appreciated, I would have to collect the information myself, do my own research, take my own photographs, and draw my own maps — eventually write my own book and convince a quality publisher to produce it.

Since that fateful day I have spent many delightful (and quite a few frustrating) hours swimming in, paddling on, and flying over this wonderful river system that has been the focus of my professional life for the past several years. Often I felt like a paddling detective going after yet another piece of evidence in the continuing effort to solve the mystery of the French River.

In this book I discuss the intricate topography of the French River as well as the presence of the thousands of travellers the river has seen over the centuries. First the Natives who were followed, early in the seventeenth century, by people from France and later from other countries. I also try to establish what canoe routes they used on their travels down and up the river. Modern trippers will then be presented with a large number of possible canoe trips that can be made on this remarkable river system.

The book is not an exhaustive, systematic study by a professional historian, but nothing more than a labor of love by a smitten paddler. Inevitably, a research project dealing with so much old and new (as well as occasionally confusing and even conflicting) material may sometimes lead to questionable conclusions. I sincerely hope that any conclusions I make may help to improve our understanding of the French River system.

Although I have tried to include as much relevant information in these pages as possible, some subjects could not be discussed due to lack of space, such as pictographs and petroglyphs, legends and myths, archaeological sites, and the origin of names. The Main Sources section, presenting the most informative of the more than two hundred sources I have consulted, may help motivate further research into these and other topics. There is a large amount of information that directly or indirectly relates the exceptional natural diversity and cultural heritage of the French River. It would be eminently worthwhile to study it more deeply than I have been able to.

We should respect and enjoy this vibrant, unusual waterway and its fragile ecosystem, and protect it from overuse and overdevelopment — do our very best to keep it healthy and thriving. May my sincere feelings for the French River be shared by many other adventurers who risk falling in love with this fascinating area that has such a glorious past.

CHRONOLOGY

Circa 800 B.C. Birth of the French River.

1535 Jacques Cartier reaches Lachine Rapids in St. Lawrence River.

2nd half 16th century Beginning of Canadian fur trade in Gulf of St. Lawrence.

1608 Samuel de Champlain establishes permanent settlement in Quebec.

Early 17th century Furs brought to New France by Indians from lands to northwest.

1609 Champlain seals alliance with Huron and Algonquin nations.

Early August 1610 Champlain sends one of his men (thought to be Etienne Brûlé) to live with Indians in interior.

Fall 1610 Likely date of first white man (Brûlé) to canoe French River.

Circa 25 June 1615 Father Le Caron leaves Lachine for Huronia.

9 July 1615 Champlain leaves Lachine for Huronia.

1 August 1615 Champlain arrives in Huronia.

From 1615 Increasing numbers of fur brought to New France by Hurons.

20 May 1616 Champlain and Father Le Caron leave Huronia for New France.

Circa 1621 First white man (probably Brûlé) to go northwest and see western Great Lakes.

1623–1624 Récollet brother Gabriel Sagard lives in Huronia.

July 1626 Jesuit priest Jean de Brébeuf comes to Huronia and leaves again before July 1629.

July 1629–March 1632 New France occupied by English.

July 1634 Jean Nicollet leaves New France to explore western Great Lakes.

5 August 1634 Brébeuf again arrives in Huronia.

1634–1640 Contagious diseases decimate Indian populations in Huronia.

1639 Beginning of construction of Ste. Marie Among the Hurons.

1640s War between Hurons and Iroquois.

1648–1649 Destruction of Huronia by Iroquois.

16 and 17 March 1649 Fathers Brébeuf and Lalemant killed by Iroquois.

14 June 1649 Ste. Marie burned down by Jesuit priests.

10 June 1650 Priests, Frenchmen, and Hurons leave for New France from Christian Island, probably by canoe via French River. End of French enterprise in Huronia.

6 August 1654 Des Groseilliers leaves New France to explore Great Lakes for new fur-producing regions.

End August 1656 Des Groseilliers returns to Quebec with many furs.

August 1659 Radisson and Des Groseilliers leave Trois-Rivières for unauthorized trip to interior.

19 August 1660 Radisson and Des Groseilliers return to Montreal from Great Lakes with fortune in furs.

2 May 1670 Hudson's Bay Company granted charter to trade in fur in all lands drained by Hudson Bay.

1730s La Vérendrye explores new lands west of Great Lakes.

Water levels marked by lines of pollen, above Dalles Rapids.

Circa 1750 French fur trade reaches pinnacle.

1754 War between France and England starts.

1760 France looses war; England occupies New France.

4 August 1761 Alexander Henry leaves Montreal for interior.

1775 Peter Pond leaves New France to explore lands northwest of Lake Superior.

1778 Peter Pond is first white man to see Methye Portage and Athabasca country.

1779 North West Company organized as loose partnership.

1783 NWC re-organized on more solid and permanent basis.

1789 Alexander Mackenzie travels Mackenzie River by canoe to Polar Sea.

1793 Alexander Mackenzie travels to Pacific Ocean by canoe.

1803 NWC inland headquarters relocated from Grand Portage to Fort Kamanistiquia.

1807 Fort Kamanistiquia renamed Fort William.

Circa 1815 Heyday of NWC.

1821 Amalgamation of NWC and HBC.

1821–1860 George Simpson governor of HBC.

1840s Silk starts to replace beaver fur as preferred material for hats.

1850 Indian Reserves (First Nations) in French River region established through signing of treaties.

1867 Canada is born.

1870s Beginning of non-native settlement in French River region.

Circa 1875 French River Village established near Main Outlet. Start of lumbering on river.

Early 1880s Lumbering takes off and remains important for more than two decades. First settlers arriving in Monetville-Noelville-Alban area. First tourists coming from North Bay.

1907–1908 Temporary dams built at Chaudière Outlets.

1908 Two railway lines built crossing French River.

Circa 1910 Lumbering business in Delta in serious decline.

1910–1916 Permanent dams built at Chaudière Outlets.

1912–1914 Big lumber companies leaving French River Village.

1922 Post office in French River Village closes.

1934 Last person leaves French River Village which is now ghost town.

1949–1950 Construction of Portage Channel and Dam.

1954 Highway 69 reaches French River and makes access much easier.

1956–1957 Dokis Road constructed.

1962 Island removed at Dalles Rapids.

1964 Rocks removed at Horseshoe Falls.

1966 Rocks removed at Horseshoe Rapids.

1968 Island and rocks removed at Little Pine Rapids.

1986 French River designated first Canadian Heritage River.

1989 Much of French River corridor made into French River Provincial Park.

1992 Portage Dam replaced by new one.

1992 Friends of French River Heritage Park established. French River Provincial Park map made and distributed.

1996 Little Chaudière Dam replaced by new one.

Lily Chutes (left) and Crooked Rapids (right) dropping into the High Cross Channel (top) in the Western Outlets, looking south.

INTRODUCTION

Listen...

Over the hard, immensely old Canadian Shield rocks of the Near North, where Ontario's huge mainland is squeezed to a narrow waist measuring a mere 160 kilometres (100 miles) from Quebec to Georgian Bay, the waters of Lake Nipissing flow westward down a most unusual waterway: the French River.

This is much more than a single stream carrying its waters from source to mouth. It is instead an intricate collection of channels and lakes, bays and marshes, rapids and falls, strategically located between the Ottawa River watershed to the east and the Great Lakes to the west. The French River shows so much physical diversity and has such a rich history that it is among the most exceptional and fascinating rivers in the province, if not Canada.

Before the arrival of Europeans in this part of the country, the Native inhabitants had used the river for countless centuries as part of a major trade route which carried them across much of northern North America. Regrettably, the name they had given the river then is lost in the mist of time; no written records survive from those prehistoric peoples.

The situation started to change dramatically in about 1610 when the first white man came from the east, followed by another some time later, then another, and still more until their light-skinned faces became a familiar sight in the region.

It was this river that brought the foreigners, Frenchmen at first, to the ancient lands and waters of the Native peoples. So the waterway soon became known in Ojibwe (the local Native language) as *Wemitigoozhi Ziibii*. *Wemitigoozhi* means stick-waver and *Ziibii* means river. This peculiar name originates from the Natives' first contact with French missionaries who were waving their crosses around while blessing the people. In time this name *Wemitigoozhi* was applied to all Frenchmen.

From then on the lives of the Natives would be changed forever, disrupted by contact with people of such a radically different culture and level of technological development.

The European visitors were explorers, missionaries, and fur traders who penetrated deeper and deeper into the unknown, eager to discover other worlds and meet new people. They travelled in birchbark canoes and were passionately dedicated to a single-minded search for knowledge, souls, or profit, willingly risking their lives in a fierce struggle to fulfil their dreams.

Over time these adventurers came to know the river by various names: Rivière des Sorcières, Rivière des Nipisiriniens, Rivière de Revillon, Rivière des François, Rivière des Français, and finally, French River.

During the more than 250 years that the western fur trade lasted, the French River formed a small-but-vital link in the lifeline between east and west. Its waters were part of the famous Champlain Trail, the Voyageurs Highway, the incredible Road to the West, a thin thread of rivers, lakes, and portages stretching for thousands of kilometres from Montreal all the way to the Pacific and Arctic Oceans.

Down this critically important but highly vulnerable canoe route, huge fortunes of precious fur were carried to ocean-going ships waiting in the St. Lawrence River, ready to transport the treasures to Europe. The backbone of this immense fur-trade network, the 4,000-kilometre-long (2,500 miles) central mainline between Montreal and Fort Chipewyan on Lake Athabasca, is shown on Map 1.

The exhilarating days of exploration, adventure, and trade are now long gone; the French River has left its glorious fur-trade past behind. No more the sweating voyageurs carrying back-breaking packs across the ancient, smooth-worn portage trails. No more the feverish rush of heavily laden canots du maître struggling upriver to get the precious furs to Montreal before the returning grip of winter would close the route down. No more the magic sound of paddlers' songs drifting over the misty stretches of the Stick-wavers' River. No more.

But perhaps they are still there somewhere, if you know how to find them, if you listen carefully with your heart. Soon you'll hear sounds coming from around the river bend: the swish of paddles, the laughter of excited voices, the water splashing against birchbark, the singing. You'll hear it all. Just close your eyes...listen...

Parmi les voyageurs, lui y a de bons enfants.
Et qui ne mangent guère, mais qui boivent souvent;
Et la pipe à la bouche, et le verre à la main,
Ils disent: camarades, versez-moi du vin.

Lorsque nous faisons rout', la charge sur le dos,
En disant: camarades, ah! grand Dieu, qu'il fait chaud!
Que la chaleur est grande! il faut nous rafraîchir;
A la fin du voyage, on prendra du plaisir.

Montreal canoe going down Devil's Door in the Western Outlets at low water, looking west.

Georgian Bay islands, smoothed by ancient glaciers.

CHAPTER 1

FRENCH RIVER SYSTEM

BIRTH OF A RIVER

Geologically speaking, the French River is still an infant, a brash young newcomer among Canada's great rivers. Let us examine some of the important events that have taken place before, during, and after the creation of the river. (The numbers cited below are approximate.)

By 23,000 B.C. the most recent ice age had started. The maximum extent of the ice sheets that covered North America (as well as other continents) was reached by 16,000 B.C.; the Laurentian Sheet extended south to the Ohio River and Long Island. The greatest thickness of the glaciers centred over Hudson Bay was about 2 kilometres (1.2 miles). At the edges they were tapered and therefore thinner.

A principal result of glaciation (other than major erosion and the tying-up of substantial amounts of global water in the form of ice) was the compression of the Precambrian bedrock of the Canadian Shield due to the elasticity of the earth's crust and the great weight of the ice. This caused the underlying rocks to sink below sea level (which was lower than today with so much water captured in glaciers).

When the climate turned warmer, the ice began to melt, the edge of the sheet retreated northward, and major glacial meltwater lakes formed at the margins of the sheet. By 12,000 B.C. the retreating ice sheet started to surrender the Great Lakes basin, marking the beginning of the evolution of the Great Lakes system. The French River area became free of ice by 10,000 B.C. and was immediately covered by the northeast arm of a huge meltwater lake (glacial Lake Algonquin). In 9000 B.C. the ice had gone from the French River area and Lake Algonquin had outlets through the French River–Mattawa Valley corridor sending the water down the Ottawa River to the ocean.

By 8000 B.C. the glaciers had withdrawn completely from the Great Lakes basin; a significant source of water was cut off and the water levels dropped rapidly. The continuing melting and lake forming was characterized by fluctuating ice fronts and great variations in size and location of the meltwater lakes. In 4000 B.C. a huge lake (glacial Lake Nipissing) covered most of the northern Great Lakes area, including the region of modern Lake Nipissing. This meltwater lake had three outlets best indicated by current names: the French River–Mattawa corridor into the Ottawa River (the main outlet); the St. Clair River into Lake Erie (a minor outlet that grew over time); and the Mississippi River through the Chicago area (also a minor outlet).

During this period the ice had long been gone from what is now the Great Lakes area. The Canadian Shield was finally free from the crushing weight of the ice and began to rebound very slowly while gradually tilting towards the southwest (different areas of the earth's crust had different rates of rise, which resulted in this tilting). In the overall context the rebounding occurred more rapidly in the beginning and then slowed down with time. Southern areas started rebounding first because they were exposed first. Their rate of rise diminished sooner so that the northern areas would catch up. The tilting land surfaces caused the northeast shores of the Great Lakes to recede, the southwest shores to become drowned, and the Lake Nipissing area to experience a slow withdrawal of water.

A sill, which would establish a drainage cutoff by forming a divide, began to rise just east of North Bay between Lake Nipissing and Trout Lake. Thus increasingly less water from the Lake Nipissing phase of the northern Great Lakes was going down the Mattawa to the east and the outflow shifted to the St. Clair River.

The water flow from the Lake Nipissing phase of the Great Lakes into the Mattawa Valley ended in 1800 B.C. with a height of land emerging at North Bay. (Other estimates give dates from 3000 to 2200 B.C. for the termination of the west-to-east flow, but 1800 B.C. is based on the most recent research by Bullock.) Current Lake Nipissing and the area that would become the French River were still part of Georgian Bay; the land kept rising and tilting to the southwest and the water levels of the northern and eastern shores of the lake fell.

Then, in 800 B.C., modern Lake Nipissing emerged from Georgian Bay and the Chaudière Rapids were formed, giving birth to the French River. For the first time, water from Lake Nipissing began flowing west instead of east, down the newly born French River, a system of ancient pre-glacial fault lines in the bedrock, which was slowly emerging from the depths of Georgian Bay. From the small rapids at Chaudière, the French River gradually increased in length as the Lake Nipissing–French River Valley rose and tilted out of Georgian Bay.

The steepness of the French River also increased over time. The rise still continues at present. North Bay rises 45–50 centimetres (17–20 inches) per century, and northeastern Georgian Bay about 35 centimetres (13 inches) per century at the mouth of the French River, somewhat less because of the differential uplift of the bedrock. Lake Nipissing is also still rising unevenly. The northeast shore of the lake rises 4–5 centimetres (1.5–2 inches) per century faster than the control point at Chaudière; the French River is tilting at about the same rate.

So the French River is gradually getting longer, steeper, and wilder; canoeists far in the future will be able to enjoy a real whitewater river.

RIVER SYSTEM OVERVIEW

The French River system consists of an elaborate group of water-filled geological fault lines running in a general east-west direction and intersected at varying angles by other rifts.

These natural formations in the Precambrian rocks make up a uniquely complex pool-and-drop network with interconnected stretches of long, narrow, flatwater lakes and relatively short lengths of current-carrying river separated by a number of constrictions. Marked by falls and rapids, these obstructions are mild much of the time but can also turn into violent, risky cataracts when the water level is high enough.

Like the Niagara River, the French River is a strait, a channel connecting two larger bodies of water. (An overview of the whole river corridor is presented on Map 2.) The water flowing down the river consists of precipitation collected in a watershed basin with a 19,100-square-kilometre (7,370 square miles) drainage area. Most of it comes out of Lake Nipissing but there are also several tributaries supplying water directly to the river. (The main ones are shown on Map 3.) The two largest tributaries are the Wanapitei and Pickerel Rivers, which empty their sometimes substantial volume into the lower reaches of the river system.

The French River begins as the southwest arm of Lake Nipissing. The lake waters drop down several rapids into two channels that together form the river proper: the Main Channel south of Okikendawt Island and the zigzagging Little French River flowing around its north side. These two channels combine west of Okikendawt Island at Wolseley Bay, but soon the waters separate again into two major channels flowing around Eighteen Mile Island, the Main Channel and the North Channel.

Close to the western end of Eighteen Mile Island, part of the Main Channel water flows down Horseshoe Bay and Deer Bay into the Pickerel River, which continues west to Ox Bay where its waters re-join those of the Main Channel.

After circling Eighteen Mile Island, which forms the central part of the French River system, the waters from the Main and North Channels come together at Dry Pine Bay. All the water coming out of Dry Pine Bay is carried west by the Main Channel into Ox Bay, which is part of the Delta where the western direction of the river abruptly changes to south–southwest.

In the Delta the river system divides into four primary outlets that, in turn, split into numerous smaller ones from which the water exits into Georgian Bay. From east to west the primary outlets are Pickerel River Outlet, Eastern Outlet, Main Outlet, and finally the Western Outlets, which are by far the most complicated of the four, carrying about two-thirds of the river's water.

The total drop of the river is 19 metres (58 feet), and its total length, measured from the beginning of the river at Frank's Point to the Black Bay–West Cross Channel intersection at the end of the Western Outlets, is 105 kilometres (66 miles). However, because of the complicated topography of the river, the combined length of all the stretches of bays, channels, and side streams that can conceivably be visited is several times greater. The area that can be explored by canoe in this elaborate waterway system increases tremendously if one is willing to portage into some of the remote lakes and streams hidden behind the banks of the river.

Although much of the river system remains as wild as it was when Natives and fur traders paddled its waters, changes brought along by the encroachment of modern society can be seen in several locations along the river such as Wolseley Bay, Eighteen Mile Bay, Dry Pine Bay, and Hartley Bay. During the second half of the last century some parts of the area were settled by immigrants for logging, fishing, and farming, adding their numbers to the Natives who were already living in the Lake Nipissing area.

Over the years, railroads and highways provided improved access to the river, and eventually tourism became the main industry. Cottages, marinas, lodges, and resorts were built, catering to adventurous visitors. (See Maps 4, 5, and 20.)

The natural flow of the river remained untouched until early this century when the need arose to control the water level of Lake Nipissing within narrow limits. The resulting dams had a direct and often unexpected effect on the water levels of the river. But there are no man-made flow-control structures or hydro dams on the river proper, so the shorelines indicated on maps are still the natural ones.

The Ladder at low water, looking north, with Double Rapids in the background.

TOPOGRAPHIC DETAILS

The complexity of the French River system makes it necessary to systematically outline the many elements of the river. I have therefore divided the system into five sections going downriver from east to west: Lake, Dokis, Island, Gorge, and Delta. (See Map 6.)

A number of detailed maps (numbers 7–18) are presented to help explain the layout of the river and its various elements. The areas outlined on these detailed maps are also shown on Map 6. Canoeists who want some additional practical information on how to handle rapids, falls, and portages will find that in Chapter 7, Suggested Canoe Trips.

One of the problems in clearly describing the river is a lack of official names for various elements of the river system. This is especially the case at the Western Outlets, and yet, the many little rapids, streams, and portages there are of great significance to canoe trippers who want to explore and enjoy these seldom-visited parts of the area. I have taken the liberty to assign names to elements I could not find official ones for, following as much as possible the example of local people, who for many years have been using several unofficial names for their own convenience.

Lake

This body of water, traditionally called the Upper French River, is a beautiful flatwater area studded with a great number of large and small islands and enriched by enchanting bays and shorelines that provide excellent settings for campsites and cottages. The main channel is quite deep in places; depths of more than 45 metres (148 feet) have been measured.

Dokis

The water coming out of the Upper French River flows around Okikendawt Island (also called Chaudière Island) in two channels, the Main Channel and the Little French River. The connection between the Upper French and these two channels is made up of six openings, five of which are natural and one man-made.

The natural ones, from east to west, are the South and North Big Chaudière Outlets, which deliver water into the Main Channel via the Upper and Lower Chaudière Rapids, and three openings dropping water into the Little French River: the Freeflowing Channel (also called Island B Channel or Island B Passage), the Little Chaudière Outlet, and the Hall Chute (the last two empty into the Little Chaudière Channel and then into the Little French River).

Dams have been built in some of these natural openings to control the water level of Lake Nipissing: two at the Big Chaudière Outlets (collectively called the Big Chaudière Dam) and one at the Little Chaudière Outlet (the Little Chaudière Dam or Little French Dam).

The man-made Portage Channel and Portage Dam were constructed southeast of the Big Chaudière Dam between Portage Bay and Bruce Bay to enable faster release of water from Lake Nipissing into the Main Channel if required.

A short distance downriver, at Keso Point, the Main Channel narrows considerably and huge standing waves may build up in Cradle Rapids (also called Cradle Falls) when the water levels are high. The Main Channel then flows for about 9 kilometres (5.6 miles) along the south shores of Okikendawt Island to Wolseley Bay (this stretch is also called Chaudière Channel).

After drawing its water from the three outlets, the Little French River flows along the north shore of Okikendawt Island. It finally drops its water into Wolseley Bay in the scenic Five Finger Rapids area via one major outlet and several secondary outlets.

Island

From Wolseley Bay the water flows down three channels: the Commanda Channel, which soon merges with the Main Channel (also called South Channel) flowing on the south side of Eighteen Mile Island, and the North Channel.

The Commanda Channel flows around three sides of Commanda Island and contains the three Rainy Rapids (First, Flat, and Third). It meets the Main Channel southeast of Big Pine Rapids.

The Main Channel continues at Little Pine Rapids, which is the first of eight rapids in the Five Mile Rapids complex. Travelling downriver, the others are Big Pine Rapids, Double Rapids, The Ladder, Blue Chute, Upper Parisien Rapids, Lower Parisien Rapids, and Crooked Rapids. The rapids are separated from each other by relatively quiet stretches of river. In this book the names Upper and Lower Parisien are used instead of Little and Big Parisien because, just as happened in previous centuries, there still appears to be a confusing lack of consensus regarding the proper names for these two rapids.

At Dalton's Point, about 16 kilometres (10 miles) below Crooked Rapids, the towers and cables of the Ontario Hydro transmission line form a reminder that the French River is, to some extent, a victim of the demands of modern technology. Here, part of the water from the Main Channel flows south into Horseshoe Bay, passes over shallow Horseshoe Rapids, and finally drops down Horseshoe Falls into the Pickerel River.

About 3 kilometres (1.9 miles) after it meets Horseshoe Bay, the Main Channel splits. Some water goes through the narrow Canoe Channel (also called Canoe Pass) into Dry Pine Bay, some is diverted south of Four Mile Island into Deer Bay and then goes down the Little French Rapids (also called Little French Cut) into a bay leading to the Pickerel River, but most of it flows south of Four Mile Island and then into Dry Pine Bay.

North of Eighteen Mile Island, the North Channel, flowing west into Eighteen Mile Bay, has three rapids: Cedar Rapids, Cedar Chute, and Ouellette Rapids. From Eighteen Mile Bay the water then drops into Dry Pine Bay via two outlets: Meshaw Falls (also called Michaud Falls) and Stony Rapids. Both Eighteen Mile Bay and Dry Pine Bay contain quite a number of cottages and permanent homes.

Montreal canoe being carried around Recollet Falls, looking west.

Gorge

Except for the water diverted to the Pickerel River, all of the water from the Main and North Channels flows out of Dry Pine Bay over The Swifts (marking the beginning of the French River Gorge) into the continuation of the Main Channel. Four kilometres (2.5 miles) down from The Swifts are the famous Recollet Falls which must be passed by taking the wooden boardwalk (first constructed in 1955) on the south side of the river.

The Recollet Falls are followed by the First Rapids and the Second Rapids (also called Little Flat Rapids) which both require extra attention only at low water levels.

The other major channel in the Gorge section is the Pickerel River. The lower section of this river is also considered part of the French River system because it carries water from the French that drops into it down Horseshoe Falls and the Little French Rapids. The Pickerel is one of the system's main tributaries.

The Main Channel and Pickerel River are crossed by three bridges, one carrying Highway 69 and the other two supporting railroad tracks.

Delta

In this final part of the river system, the waters coming down from the entire watershed spread out in a delightful patchwork of channels, outlets, and exits to meet the waiting waves of Georgian Bay. The Delta is the most complicated and diverse section of the French River. Its wild shores have the least amount of modern development and beg to be explored, revealing much of the country as it was long ago when the fur traders were passing through in their birchbark canoes.

In the northern half of the Delta the waters from the Main Channel and the Pickerel River combine with the sometimes substantial flow from the Wanapitei River. The major bodies of water here are Ox Bay, Hartley Bay, and Wanapitei Bay, which contain the core of modern boating and cottage activities in the area.

From Wanapitei Bay and Ox Bay down to the south-southwest, several large and small faults in the rock form a unique fan-shaped complex of channels. Three of those channels lead to three primary outlets, which in turn divide into several exits out of which the waters finally drop into Georgian Bay. A fourth channel–outlet combination going south from the Pickerel River comes into existence when the water level in the Delta is high enough.

This whole area is collectively called the mouth of the French River, although it is in fact made up of a multitude of openings. The number of final exits coming from the four major outlets (Pickerel River, Eastern, Main, and Western) is about fourteen, depending upon the water level of the river.

The Pickerel River Outlet gets most of its water from the Pickerel River. This outlet divides into the East Channel and the West Channel. Both contain several rapids and exit into a long, north-pointing arm of Georgian Bay.

The Eastern Outlet is located at the end of the Canoe Channel below Bass Lake, where the two small exits of Bass Creek, Bass Creek Falls and Bass Creek West Exit, drop the water into the Bay. Around 1910, in order to bypass these rapids, a tramway was built in this location by the local lumber company, enabling them to move their mills from French River Village to another spot up the Pickerel River (see Chapter 5). In later years this narrow-gauge tramway was replaced with a wooden walkway. The present boardwalk was rebuilt in 1989 by the Ministry of Natural Resources and is now commonly used to transport boats, canoes, and other equipment and material between the French River proper and Georgian Bay. In 1929 the Department of Lands and Forests tried to make a bypass southeast of the tramway by blasting a rock ridge and installing rails and a small car, making use of an existing stretch of water. However, this bypass was only used for a short while and then abandoned.

The Main Outlet is found at the end of the Main Channel where most of the water goes down the deeper channel on the south side of the Dalles Rapids. At very low water, however, all the water stays left, exposing an ugly expanse of jagged rocks left behind after the removal of an island from the middle of the river in 1962. Below these major rapids the water flows into the Dalles Pool and then finally down the mild Little Dalles Rapids into Georgian Bay.

Finally, at the end of the Western Channel are the Western Outlets. These have a delta of their own with a complicated and intriguing pattern of channels, outlets, and exits. The Western Outlets are made up of three outlet systems which are, from the east, the Bad River Channel, the Old Voyageur Channel, and the Voyageur Channel. (See the composite aerial photograph on page 91.)

The Bad River Channel consists of a pair of secondary channels, Boat Channel and Otter Channel (which continue as West Branch and East Branch), and divides its waters in a series of outlets: Herring Chute, Lily Chutes, Crooked Rapids (the second set of this name on the river), which ends in The Jump, and Back Channel, Lovers Lane, and Herb's Channel.

All the outlets of the Bad River Channel drop their water into the High Cross Channel. From

The first paddle of the day.

the High Cross Channel the water finally flows into Georgian Bay via several exits: Devil's Door, Little and Big Jameson Rapids (also called Little and Big Jamieson Rapids), the two Harris Rapids, and Cross Channel Rapids (which drop water westward into the West Cross Channel).

The second major channel of the Western Outlets is the Old Voyageur Channel, which was part of one of the French River canoe routes in the fur-trade era. There are four locations in this channel that require close study regarding its usefulness as part of a canoe route. The first one of these is the Rock Circus, where the water coming from the north divides into two parts: much of it flows down the East Channel, a narrow, fairly straight passage on the east side, and the rest goes into the wider, more complicated section to the west. The East Channel and the Rock Circus are connected by several openings enabling water to flow between them. The water level must be reasonably high for canoes to be able to navigate the East Channel comfortably.

A short distance further some of the channel's water drops over the Boston Falls to the south into Mills Channel and then, via Shannon Bay, to the West Cross Channel.

The Old Voyageur Channel itself continues on, passing picturesque Morse Bay to the south. It then gets to the second obstruction, the well-known Petite Faucille (Little Sickle), a small lift-over rapid, less than a metre (3 feet) high, mentioned several times in the old fur-trade literature.

About 300 metres (990 feet) below Petite Faucille, the Palmer Rocks cross the channel at an angle that can make this passage difficult to negotiate if the water is too low.

The last section of the Old Voyageur Channel is a fairly straight, 100-metre-long (330 feet) passage running between two 4–5-metre-wide (13–16 feet), 15-metre-high (50 feet) sloping rock walls. Going down it at high water is a sheer delight because of the considerable speed at which the water rushes through. This must be La Dalle, the Trough or Gutter that over the years has seen so many travellers go down and up its picturesque channel. The Old Voyageur Channel soon meets the West Cross Channel, providing a clear passage to Georgian Bay.

The last of the Western Outlets is the Voyageur Channel. It gets some of its water from the narrow, steep-walled Mushroom Channel that runs below several small falls at its north end. To the west of this little channel is a relatively flat, now heavily treed area that might have been used in the past as a portage to get canoes down into the channel proper. However, this may have been just a convenient place to move logs downriver during the logging times. The rest of the water for the Voyageur Channel enters over the Marten Cut, a man-made opening in a long rocky ridge separating the channel proper from the upper part of the Western Outlets. Water only flows down the Voyageur Channel when river water levels are reasonably high.

The short stretch just before the mouth of the Voyageur Channel, called Stamp Channel, is the only part of the whole French River system with waters flowing due north. It gets its name from a 1994 Canada Post stamp celebrating the Routes of the Fur Traders. The stamp was based on a photo taken here in 1989.

The Voyageur Channel drops into Black Bay via Heron Bay and then through a narrow passage called the Washer Woman (after a woman said to have operated a laundry near here during the logging years). At high river water level the Washer Woman shows a considerable hydraulic step that can be difficult to negotiate when travelling upstream. If the Georgian Bay level is very high its water can go up into Heron Bay and fill the Voyageur Channel, making this channel navigable even if the river water level is very low.

On maps, the Voyageur Channel looks tempting as a possible canoe route as it is shorter than the others. However, this channel is very hard to access at low river water levels, especially using large canoes. It seems, therefore, somewhat out of place to call this the Voyageur Channel since it is unlikely that fur-trade freight canoes would have used this channel on a regular basis given the great difficulties that would have been encountered.

Black Bay is directly connected to Georgian Bay via the Fort Channel and also via the west-going West Cross Channel, which is part of the Cross Channel, a curious fault running east–west through the western part of the Delta and cutting the above-mentioned north–south outlet channels at almost right angles.

On the south shore of the West Cross Channel, close to Black Bay, there is a peculiar collection of tumbled-down rocks where several circular openings seem to have been constructed. This was possibly used as a shelter by Natives lying in ambush for the treasure-filled fur-trade canoes that would pass down the channel, which is quite narrow at this point. This could well be the "Fort" talked about in some old reports and after which the Fort Channel was named.

At the far western end of the West Cross Channel, called Indian Bay, is the probable location of the Prairie des Français (also called Grand Prairie). Here, in the fur-trade times, brigades of freight canoes would wait out the bad weather before moving on to Georgian Bay, giving the travellers the opportunity to attend to their canoes and freight during the short period of rest. It is a reasonably large and flat expanse of land that can accommodate quite a number of tents and large canoes.

The northeastern part of Georgian Bay that lies within the French River Provincial Park boundaries and into which the many exits of the French River empty its waters is a very scenic area filled with countless islands, rocks, and shoals, and crowned by the renowned Bustard Islands.

WATER LEVELS

To understand the French River one must understand the processes governing the behavior of its water levels.

When water flows from Lake Nipissing and the river's tributaries into the French River system, a complex mechanism is set in motion. This mechanism deserves considerable study because it concerns many interests such as commercial navigation, cottaging, boating, canoeing, and sport fishing, and environmental issues such as water quality, fish habitat, waterfowl nesting, flooding, ice damage, water intakes, and sewage outfalls.

The water level of the river is determined by the amount of precipitation that falls in the watershed, by the amount of evaporation and plant and soil absorption, and by the flow characteristics of the channels through which the water moves.

A change in lake water level has a much more noticeable effect on the river than it has on Lake Nipissing because the river has a much smaller surface area to accommodate the same change in volume. For instance, letting a depth of 1 centimetre (0.4 inches) of water flow from the lake into the river in one day will raise the river level in the Dry Pine Bay area by approximately 48 centimetres (19.2 inches). So, the river system behaves somewhat like a living entity, pulsating and breathing, expanding and contracting, in rhythm with the amount of water being fed into its body.

Until the early 1900s, the flow of water through the system was part of a natural process that did not feel the hand of man; there was no interference, no control. The water level was a direct and immediate result of the amount and distribution of precipitation. But because of the lack of sufficient and accurate information we do not know what that precipitation was before that time. It is therefore impossible to give a faithful account of what happened during those seasons; we can only make educated guesses at the water level changes.

The following is an attempt to describe a typical cycle of the water level variations of Lake Nipissing before control measures were initiated in the early 1900s (all elevations are in reference to the Geodetic Survey of Canada vertical reference elevation):

By the end of March, the water level would drop to a winter low of about 194.5 metres

(638 feet), maybe lower. In April and May the lake would fill with rain and melted snow and by the end of April the ice would begin to leave the lake. By early June, the summer high of about 197.2 metres (647 feet) or more would be reached, depending upon the amount of winter snow cover. In June, July, and August the level would drop quickly at first and then gradually to the summer low which could get as low as about 195.7 metres (642 feet). During the summer, the evaporation caused by high temperatures and low humidity would have been a contributing factor in determining the water level. In the fall there would be some increase in the water level because of rain, followed by a slight decrease to the early winter level. Ice would form on the lake by mid-December. During the winter there would be a steady draw-down of the water level to the winter low at the end of March.

Historically then, Lake Nipissing fluctuated considerably between extremes. There may have been a difference of 1.5 metres (5 feet) or more between the highest level after the spring freshet in April and the lowest summer level in July or August. The maximum fluctuation between winter low and spring high may have been around 2.7 metres (9 feet). Lake Nipissing had higher lows during wet times and could be virtually dry in periods of drought. The overall spring water level was probably higher and the overall summer level considerably lower than in the present-day controlled situation.

Fluctuations in the river water level followed those of Lake Nipissing. The peak river flows were much higher than today because of the lack of control of the lake level so that the river water levels would have been higher in the spring and lower in summer and fall. Canoeists paddling the French River before the early 1900s would have been highly dependent upon the water levels of both Lake Nipissing and the river. They would have had to deal with these larger fluctuations.

Beginning in the 1880s, very ambitious plans were made to build the Georgian Bay Ship Canal from Montreal to Georgian Bay using the channels of the Ottawa River, the Mattawa River, Lake Nipissing, and the French River. This canal would have required sufficient depth for large freighters to navigate Lake Nipissing and therefore some form of control was needed to counteract the lake's low summer water levels. The intention was to achieve this control by means of dams, which would regulate the flow through three of the five natural outlets of Lake Nipissing into the French River.

Although these canal plans were eventually abandoned in favor of the more economical Welland Canal in the Niagara Peninsula, the control dams were built anyway to keep the water

Canoeing class at Blue Chute.

level in Lake Nipissing high enough for summer navigation by other boat traffic, as well as to help the lumber industry move its log rafts.

(From the early 1800s to today there have been at least ten proposals that would have turned large parts of the French River into a lock-regulated canal of some sort. We may be thankful that none of these plans has succeeded, because any of them would have irreparably destroyed the natural beauty of the river system.)

All in all, from 1907 until the late 1960s, significant waterflow control measures were taken on Lake Nipissing and the French River itself. Initially little or no attention was paid to the effects that control of the lake might have on the French River system below the dams. The earliest constructions were made to regulate the flow of water from Lake Nipissing into the river. In 1907 and 1908, temporary cribwork dams were built at the main Big Chaudière Outlets and at the Little French River Outlet, giving some water-level control, which would be required to build permanent dams. Between 1910 and 1916, the permanent Big and Little Chaudière Dams were constructed in the present locations. The Portage Channel and the Portage Dam southeast of the Big Chaudière Dam were built from 1949 to 1950 with the intent to provide a measure of flood control on Lake Nipissing, to improve the lowering of the lake during the winter months in preparation for spring run-off, and to improve navigation on the lake. In 1992, the Portage Dam was replaced by a new, electronically controlled dam. In 1996 the Little Chaudière Dam was also replaced by a new one.

The building of the Portage Channel (also called the Spillway) destroyed a considerable part of the Chaudière Portage, which had been a short-but-crucial link in the continental east–west canoe route used by the Natives, fur traders, and others.

With these constructions Lake Nipissing has become a regulated water body. Its water level is determined by management strategies using sophisticated computer-based control procedures that take many factors into consideration. Instead of the natural 1.5-metre (five feet) change between spring high and summer low, the level of Lake Nipissing is now kept within 20 centimetres (8 inches), between 195.75 metres and 195.95 metres, during the summer navigation season (mid-May to early October). Normally the operating values are set by on-site personnel, but if necessary they can be adjusted electronically from Toronto by remote control. The Chaudière and Portage Dams are owned and operated by Public Works and Government Services Canada.

All of these measures were taken to regulate the water level of Lake Nipissing but they also directly affect the water level in the French River system. Lag times between the opening of the dams and the changes in river water levels downstream vary. At Wolseley Bay the lag time is between half a day and a day, at Dry Pine Bay, between two-and-a-half and five days, and at Hartley Bay, between three-and-a-half and six days.

In the 1960s some efforts were made to directly control the river water levels. The purpose of these local changes in the waterway was to provide an extra measure of flood control by increasing the flow during spring high water, by facilitating faster removal of ice dams, and by reducing water-level fluctuations. A ten-percent increase in the discharge capacity of the river was hoped to be reached through rock excavation at major constrictions. In 1962 about 1 metre (3 feet) was removed off the top of a rock island at Dalles Rapids, considerably lowering the high water level in the Delta. In 1964 some rocks were cleared from the channel at Horseshoe Falls. In 1966 a rock obstruction was removed at Horseshoe Rapids. In 1968 about 1.5 metres (5 feet) were removed off the top of a rock island in the river at Little Pine Rapids as well as some rocks on the west shore. (The 1968 alterations in the Little French Rapids were not made to increase the discharge capacity of the outlet, but to help control the lamprey population.) Several other minor measures were also taken: some rocks were removed at Ouellette Rapids, the Marten Cut was blasted at the north entrance of the Voyageur Channel, and the channel was deepened at the Bass Creek West Exit.

Some of these channel "improvement" measures were not entirely welcome as they brought along substantial and often unwanted changes in water level in the areas above and below the sites. These changes usually had unexpected consequences for fish spawning, navigation, boating, canoeing, beaches, and cottages. The removal of the Dalles Rapids island, for example, resulted in a greater high-water outflow down this channel and hence a marked decrease in high-water levels in the whole Delta, including the four major outlets. In several cases (for instance at Little Pine Rapids and Horseshoe Rapids) the rock excavations also left ugly piles of rock debris lying at or near the removal site.

The Delta and a major part of the Gorge section are subject to an important local phenomenon: the water levels of these sections are greatly influenced by inflow from the Wanapitei and Pickerel Rivers, which at times can be very high, occasionally contributing to a difference of 4 metres (13 feet) between minimum and maximum water levels.

The amount of river-water outflow from the many exits into Georgian Bay is not controlled by the water level of the Bay itself. High or low Bay levels can, however, have considerable influ-

Double Rapids at low water, looking northwest.

ence on the conditions of some of the exits and hence upon the quality and size of the exit rapids and falls.

FLORA AND FAUNA

During the last ice age, the repeated action of glaciers moving over the Canadian Shield had scraped the rocks clean of its layer of soil. The entire pre-glaciation flora and fauna of the French River area, therefore, had either been destroyed by the relentless scouring of the ice sheets or was displaced southward. Locally, nutrient-poor sediment and rock rubble had been pushed into hollows and cracks in the rocks, making pockets of habitat for new plant growth.

When the area finally became free of ice about eleven thousand years ago, a new community of living things started to develop in the barren world. The first plants to grow in this tundra, characterized by a cold climate and permafrost, were primitive, pioneering lichens that slowly broke down the rocks, creating soil for higher plants to live in. This phase was followed by the growth of a subarctic–boreal forest community with sterile soils and cool climate (as it was still relatively close to the receding ice sheet).

As the glaciers retreated further northward and the climate became warmer, other plants gradually moved in, followed by animals including caribou, elk, and arctic fox (and possibly now-extinct species such as mammoth, mastodon, giant beaver, and woolly rhinoceros). These animals were soon followed by people.

The continually modifying distribution of flora and fauna was greatly influenced by the varying sizes and locations of glacial meltwater lakes, the changing climate, the continuing erosion of the landscape, and the rebound of glacially depressed rocks. It took the French River area about five thousand years (till about 4000 B.C.) to develop the vegetation it contains today.

The modern vegetation of the French River area is mixed forest characterized by contact between the northern boreal forest and the deciduous forest to the south. This transitional forest is dominated by the coniferous white pine, red pine, jack pine, white spruce, cedar, and hemlock, and the deciduous red maple, sugar maple, yellow birch, aspen, beech, red oak, and basswood. The proximity of Georgian Bay has a marked influence on the distribution of plant species across the area.

A particularly noteworthy plant is the Virginia chain fern. At the French River the fern is at the northwestern range limit for its species in Ontario; it is more abundant in eastern Canada. The fern is found throughout the French River area but is most abundant at the mouth.

The animal population of the French River area consists of species such as moose, white-tailed deer, black bear, beaver, fox, raccoon, rabbit, skunk, marten, mink, muskrat, porcupine, mouse, red squirrel, chipmunk, snakes, turtles, frogs, and many species of bird such as raven, great blue heron, common loon, ducks, gulls, and other shore birds, song birds, and waterfowl. Other, less-abundant-to-rare species include wolf, lynx, fisher, otter, flying squirrel, salamander, turkey vulture, pine warbler, double-crested cormorant, osprey, caspian tern, eastern bluebird, Brewer's blackbird, and bald eagle.

Two species that exist in the Delta deserve special attention: the wapiti and the Massasauga rattlesnake. The wapiti (elk) are remnants of a herd that was reintroduced to this area in the early 1930s and has been protected from hunting since 1978. The self-sustaining wapiti population, estimated at a stable twenty-five animals, probably spends the fall and winter around King's Island south of the Western Channel.

White trillium.

The eastern massasauga rattlesnake is Ontario's only poisonous snake, a threatened species and protected by law. With luck this small and rather timid snake can be found around the Delta and the offshore islands in Georgian Bay, where it hunts frogs and mice. It is not an aggressive snake and should be left alone in its habitat. There are several other species such as the eastern garter snake, the northern water snake, the fox snake, and the milk snake, which are harmless and should not be disturbed.

It is possible that a few bison still roam the lands west and north of the Delta. If they do, they are all that is left of a small herd that was re-introduced to the area in 1930 along with the wapiti. The last time a bison was seen in the area was in 1983 and the herd is now thought to be extinct.

For a long time the French River system has been famous for its sport fishing, the most prized fish to catch being pickerel (walleye), pike, bass, muskie, and sturgeon. In the last few decades, because of overharvesting, the heavy pressure on the fish population has created a situation in which the tourism industry has become threatened by the lack of adequate numbers and quality of game fish. Since the early 1990s concerted efforts have been made to remedy this problem through programs to improve spawning habitat, by stocking and developing viable fish populations, and by implementing regulations on the size and number of fish kept. Efforts are also made to fine tune the control of water levels by incorporating sophisticated systems to adjust the setting of the control dams in such a manner that all parties involved with the river are satisfied. These measures are showing good results and the future of the French River as a first-class sport-fishing paradise again looks promising.

Little Pine Rapids at very high water, looking south.

CHAPTER 2

NATIVE PEOPLES

The first people to move into the lands that had been freed from the cover of ice about eleven thousand years ago were probably the Paleo-Indians, primitive hunters–gatherers who followed animals such as caribou that grazed upon the lichen and other plants growing in the tundra. Very little is known about these early visitors to the French River area. They used knives and axes made from stone and utensils made from wood, stone, bone, and horn.

Over the centuries, more people came as the ice retreated further north and larger numbers of animals moved in, but there is little information on these stone-age indigenous populations because no written records exist. Up to the arrival of the Europeans into these parts early in the seventeenth century very little is known of the lives of the original inhabitants.

By about A.D. 1600, an estimated 65,000 Native people were living in the primeval forest of what is now Southern Ontario, many of them in the region between Lake Simcoe and southern Georgian Bay called Huronia. The few Natives that lived in the French River area were mostly Algonquins. West of the French River lived the Ottawa Ojibwa and around Lake Nipissing and the upper French River lived the semi-nomadic Nipissing (all belonging to the Algonkian linguistic family).

The Native population of Georgian Bay's northeastern shore probably included a few rather isolated nomadic family groups or bands that moved from one hunting or fishing ground to another. South of them lived nations of the Iroquoian linguistic family, from southern Georgian Bay down to what is now northern New York State including the Hurons living northwest of Lake Simcoe.

The French River was part of an extensive network of waterways along which people travelled in birchbark canoes, trading in many goods such as pendants made of conch from the Gulf of Mexico, beads from Atlantic Coast shells, copper from Lake Superior, and flints from other regions. In the early seventeenth century trade in furs also started to develop with the Europeans who had recently settled on the shores of the Gulf of St. Lawrence.

The Huron Indians soon became important middlemen in this fur trade. They regularly transported great loads of fur in large flotillas of many dozens of canoes, from Huronia up the French

Looking upstream from Double Rapids toward Big Pine Rapids.

River to the European settlements in the east, to trade for European goods, which they then took back for trading with other Indian nations.

This trade eventually had a devastating influence on the Natives, completely disrupting their traditional lives. They became more and more dependent upon the Europeans, losing many of their beliefs and customs; large numbers were converted to the European religion. Especially disastrous was the introduction of foreign sicknesses such as chicken pox, scarlet fever, tuberculosis, and other epidemic diseases leading to a large reduction in Native population.

In 1648 and 1649 the Hurons in the Lake Simcoe area were attacked and defeated by the Iroquois from the south, who wanted to control the lucrative fur trade and were looking for new territories from which to collect fur as their own sources were becoming depleted. Nipissing to the north were also attacked because they were trading partners of the Hurons.

Native involvement in several wars between the French and the English was another factor in the widening split between the various Indian nations. The northern nations, some of which were from the Iroquoian family, allied themselves with the French, while the southern Iroquois nations allied themselves with the British. The main reason for all this turmoil was a struggle for control of the country's all-important waterways, which were the only trade routes in existence connecting the remote parts of the ever-expanding French (and later British) fur empire.

Ontario was the main hub of canoe travel in the northern part of North America and the strategically located French River was a busy waterway indeed. There are very few direct signs of all this human activity along the French River, but several pictograph sites, possibly hundreds of years old, have been identified. Unfortunately, most of the drawings are not easily decipherable.

By the mid-1800s, the French–British–Indian wars were long past and the Natives lived peacefully, mostly subsisting on agriculture, hunting, and fishing. However, the interest by European settlers in the lands occupied by several of the Indian bands escalated due to the increasing importance of lumbering in the vast forests and of valuable minerals that were discovered in the ancient Canadian Shield rocks. Treaties were signed with the Natives, establishing Indian Reserves. In the French River area this took place in 1850.

Two reserves are directly connected with the French River: the Dokis First Nation (Indian Reserve 9) in the upper part of the river, and the French River First Nation (Indian Reserve 13) just east of Highway 69. At present the Ojibwa population in each of the two First Nations is around two hundred, many of them making a living through tourism, lumbering, or fishing.

*Pulling the canoe down a
shallow side channel south of
Wanapitei Bay at low water.*

CHAPTER 3

FRENCH PERIOD (UNTIL 1760)

EARLY FUR TRADE

When Jacques Cartier sailed up the St. Lawrence River in 1535 in his futile search for a route to the fabled fortunes of Asia, the seas off Newfoundland had already been visited for years by boats from western Europe fishing the immensely rich Grand Banks and other areas, mainly for cod.

In the second half of the sixteenth century, the English were gradually forcing other fishermen away from the waters south of Newfoundland to different parts of the coast and to the Gulf of St. Lawrence. French fishermen and Basque whalers occasionally had contact with the Natives living on the shores of the Gulf. This led to small-scale trading where European goods such as clothes, beads, cooking pots, tools, and weapons were bartered for the Indian's beaver-fur robes, which were in great demand in Europe where they could be sold for large profits.

As the European market for fur grew quickly during the latter half of the century, this small-scale trading developed into a better-organized system involving well-financed groups of French merchants who tried to get hold of as much of the precious fur as possible. More and more Indians came down in their birchbark canoes from the back-country to the trading places at the mouths of the rivers emptying into the St. Lawrence River and the Gulf, carrying increasingly larger quantities of fur, mainly beaver, to trade for the much-sought-after European goods. Inevitably the local sources of fur-bearing animals became depleted and new ones had to be found.

In 1608 Samuel de Champlain established the Habitation in what is now Quebec, the first permanent French settlement in North America. This was done in an effort to create a new French colony and also to tap and control vast new sources of fur and to organize the fur trade on a more profitable level to satisfy the steadily growing demand of the European fashion industry.

Indeed, fashion was the sole driving force behind the fur trade that would play such a central role in the development of North America and eventually in the creation of Canada. The demand for beaver pelts was especially immense because the soft underfur was ideally suited to make waterproof, shiny, strong, but still extremely soft felt. The felt could be shaped into a variety of stylish and expensive hats that would be worn by men of quality, emphasizing their rank and status.

This fascination with felt hats started in the middle of the sixteenth century and lasted for an incredible three hundred years until they were gradually replaced by cheaper hats made of silk. What makes the beaver's fur so suitable for the production of felt are the tiny serrations (also called barbs or teeth) on the hairs of its under-layer of soft wool. When the fur is treated by pressure and hot water or steam, the hairs will interlock tightly and permanently, creating excellent felting.

It is humbling to consider that, without these little serrations on the beaver's hair, Canada might have been a quite different kind of country.

EXPLORERS AND MISSIONARIES

Early in the seventeenth century, furs from the Indian nations in the north and the west were brought to the European traders on the St. Lawrence River by various Native tribes who, over the centuries, had developed a role as middlemen in the trade among the Indians. The Hurons (Wendat), living about 150 kilometres (94 miles) southeast of the mouth of the French River in heavily populated Huronia (Wendake) between Georgian Bay and Lake Simcoe, were experienced trade specialists. They often had to deal with Algonquin tribes living along the Ottawa River who could demand that toll be paid on goods passing through their territory.

After 1609, and especially from about 1615 on, the Hurons loaded their canoes with fur they had obtained from other tribes who were living in the distant interior, and followed the trade route to the east. This increasingly important canoe route went along the east coast of Georgian Bay, then followed the French River upstream, crossed Lake Nipissing, traversed the LaVase Portages to Trout Lake, went down the Mattawa River, and finally followed the Ottawa River to the trading centres in New France.

The years between 1610 and 1650 would prove to be of great significance to the French River because of the major events taking place in Huronia that had a direct and important bearing on what happened on the river itself. These four decades would see the beginnings of the fur trade from the west, the first white explorers and traders, the first fleets loaded with trade goods and fur, the first contact between Huron Indians and European missionaries preaching their alien religion, the horrific ravages of disease that killed thousands, and the first European settlement in

Big Pine Rapids at very high water, looking east.

the interior of New France. Then, finally, there would be the wholesale slaughter brought on by a vicious war between Indian nations that would tear apart the lives of tens of thousands of Natives, killing great numbers and destroying their country and way of life.

In all this, the French River played an essential role as a strategically located water highway carrying great quantities of canoes back and forth between the two centres of activity: Quebec in the east and Huronia in the west.

In 1609 Samuel de Champlain, who was the governor of New France, sealed an alliance with the Huron and Algonquin nations that led to the first few furs being brought down the Ottawa River to the French merchants in Quebec by the Natives.

In the early days of August 1610, Champlain, wanting more control of the fur trade, sent one of his men to go and live with the Natives of the interior to establish a strong relationship with them by learning their language and way of life. Champlain's main goal was to achieve a better understanding of their operations, which he hoped would improve the trade in furs. He also wanted to increase his knowledge of the country further west, as he was still eager to find a road to the Orient and its fabulous riches.

It is generally assumed that the man Champlain sent out, who went with a group of Algonquins to their villages on the Ottawa River, was eighteen-year-old Etienne Brûlé. Many of these Algonquins regularly travelled to Huronia, where they spent the winter with the Huron Indians. Brûlé would likely have accompanied them in the fall of 1610 on their annual trip to Huronia via the Mattawa and French Rivers and the eastern shores of Georgian Bay.

If this were the case, Brûlé was the first non-Indian to travel the French River, guided by his adoptive Native friends, over many of the same trails and portages we use today.

Brûlé stayed with the Indians for less than a year and returned to Lachine about 13 June 1611 in a party with two hundred Natives, going back with them to their homes later in the season. Brûlé probably lived with the Indians, among them the Hurons, until 1615 and would have travelled the French River several times when he accompanied Indian fur-trade fleets on the annual trips to and from New France. Unfortunately, there are few records of Brûlé's activities; he left no written account of his many travels. Most of what we know about him is found in Champlain's writings but Brûlé's name is rarely mentioned.

It is likely that Brûlé was followed by several other young white men wanting to learn the Indian way of life and encourage the Indians to trade, as well as by individual fur traders who would go into the interior on their own initiative.

In 1615 Champlain decided to go west himself to strengthen the bonds with the Hurons and maintain a healthy trading partnership with them. However, about 25 June 1615, two weeks before Champlain could go, the Récollet Father Joseph Le Caron left Lachine for Huronia in great urgency with twelve French soldiers, accompanying the returning Huron fur fleet. The zealous but inexperienced friar was leaving on such short notice because he had made it his mission "to be the first to proclaim the name of God to the red men, and if need be, to suffer somewhat for the name and glory of our Saviour Christ." He was determined to reach his "parish" as quickly as possible and to spend the winter there. Le Caron was probably not the first white man to see the French River but his is the first name documented as having travelled the French River to Huronia.

Two weeks after Le Caron, on 9 July 1615, Champlain finally left Lachine and paddled up the Ottawa River, possibly with Brûlé as guide and interpreter, another young Frenchman who might have been a valet, and ten Hurons, all in two heavily loaded canoes. The party went down the French River in late July, travelled the east coast of Georgian Bay, and arrived in Huronia on

Solo paddler in Blue Chute.

1 August, having taken twenty-three days (twenty days of actual travelling) for the 850-kilometre (530 miles) trip. (See Map 19.)

Champlain was the first European to draw maps of the area he travelled through and also the first to produce a written journal of his many trips. These are his own words in seventeenth-century French, the first ever written about the French River:

Apres nous auoir reposé deux iours auec le chef desdits Nipisierinij: nous nous rembarquasmes en nos canaux, & entrames dans vne riuire, par où ce lac se descharge, & fismes par icelle quelques trente-cinq lieuës, & descendismes par plusieurs petits saults, tant par terre, que par eau, iusques au lac Attigouautan. Tout ce païs est encores plus malaggreable que le precedent, car ie n'y ay point veu le long d'iceluy dix arpents de terre labourable, sinon rochers, & païs aucunement montagneux.

which means,

Having rested two days with the chief of the said Nipissings, we re-embarked in our canoes and entered a river flowing out of this lake, and made some thirty-five leagues along it, and passed several little rapids, some by portaging, others by running them, as far as Lake Attigouautan [Georgian Bay]. This whole region is even more unprepossessing than the former; for I did not see in the whole length of it ten acres of arable land, but only rocks and a country somewhat hilly. (Biggar 1922, vol. 3:42)

Champlain stayed with the Hurons for less than ten months, learning much about their way of life and helping them attack their constant rivals and enemies, the Iroquois, who were living to the south in what is now upstate New York. On 20 May 1616, he left Huronia to return to Lachine together with Le Caron and the French soldiers and the Huron fur fleet, again via the French River. He arrived at the St. Lawrence about the end of June.

The direct result of Champlain's voyage was an improved relationship with the Hurons and an increased fur trade. After 1615, fleets of Huron fur canoes regularly travelled the French and Ottawa Rivers en route to New France, each year bringing ten thousand or more beaver skins to the French traders as well as other furs.

In all these activities the French River played a crucial role as part of the most direct link between east and west. It truly had become the gateway to a new country where not only great fortunes could be made by the fur traders, but also many souls could be "saved" by the religious men from France. These missionaries came to the Indian lands to obsessively follow their calling to teach the "savages" the blessings of conversion to Christianity, which proved to be of questionable value to the Natives.

The first missionary to work in what is now Ontario was the above-mentioned Father Le Caron who stayed in Huronia during parts of 1615 and 1616 and again from 1623–1624. From 1617 until 1622 there were no missionaries in Huronia.

Between 1622 and 1628, a few other Récollet friars travelled the French River on their way to and from Indian country. The best known of these was Gabriel Sagard, a Récollet lay brother who lived in Huronia for about a year in 1623 and 1624.

In July 1626, the Jesuit priest Jean de Brébeuf also came to Huronia via the French River and stayed until he was called back to Quebec in haste just before the British occupied the country in July 1629. During this occupation, which would last till March 1632, the fur trade with the Hurons was apparently run by English and Scottish merchants, now at a smaller scale because few Huron visited the colony. The Hurons did not get along well with the new European traders. Between 1629 and 1634, there again were no missionaries in Huronia.

In 1632 the trade between the French and the Hurons took off once more and the activities on the French River increased. From 1633 until 1649, many Huron fur flotillas, ranging from a few to as many as 150 canoes with 700 men, travelled the French River on their long and dangerous journey to and from New France. The traffic jams caused by the long lines of canoes with men and cargo trying to get across the narrow portages as fast as possible must have been an incredible sight and a very frustrating experience.

On 7 July 1634, Brébeuf again left Trois-Rivières, on the St. Lawrence River, for Huronia where he arrived on 5 August. From then on the Jesuits, whom the Indians called "Black Robes," were in sole command of the Huron mission.

Disaster struck around 1634 when contagious diseases, to which the Indians had little resistance, were accidentally introduced from Quebec via the French River into the Great Lakes region, decimating the Huron population to less than half its original size over the next six years.

In 1639, the Jesuits decided to build a permanent fortified mission on the banks of the Wye River near present-day Midland. Saint Marie Among the Hurons eventually consisted of more than twenty buildings, including a church, chapel, hospital, smithy, carpenter shop, farm, granary, kitchen, bunkhouse, stables, residences, and soldiers' barracks.

This settlement was occupied at times by up to sixty Frenchmen including Jesuit priests (eighteen of them in 1647), donnés (volunteer lay helpers), domestic servants, a mason, a car-

*Narrow East Channel of
the Pickerel River Outlet,
looking north.*

penter, a cabinet maker, a blacksmith, a druggist, a barber, a surgeon, a tailor, a shoemaker, cat-echist-helpers (boys between ten and sixteen years of age), and soldiers. There were no women in Huronia.

The thin and vulnerable lifeline that connected Ste. Marie to Montreal (established in 1642) was about 850 kilometres (530 miles) long and had to be travelled by canoe via the French-Ottawa route, which saw quite a lot of traffic in these years. Going all the way to Quebec City down the St. Lawrence River added another 250 kilometres (160 miles) of paddling.

An amazingly diverse assortment of people and goods was transported back and forth over the waters and portages of the French River. The priests and other Frenchmen had to find not only their own place in the 6.1- to 7.6-metre-long (20–25 feet) Huron fur trade canoes, but also room for farm animals (calves, pigs, and poultry), religious paraphernalia (including vestments, altar covers, crucifixes, chalices, ornaments, candelabras, candles, bibles, hosts, and wine), a church bell, tools of all kinds, smithy material (such as raw iron, copper, brass, and a 1-metre-long (3 feet) bellows), 20-kilogram (44 pounds) bronze pharmaceutical mortars, venetian glass bottles, square glass bottles for wine and spirits transported together in crates, glazed earthenware, kitchen equipment, cutlery, furnishings, a clock, lanterns, rolls of cloth, blankets, clothes, medicines and instruments for the hospital, food stores (including seeds and dried fruit), books, reports and writ-ten correspondence, writing tools (parchment, paper, pens, and ink), trinkets and weapons for the Indians, bales of fur, trade goods, weapons and equipment for the soldiers, and more. These canoe fleets were often quite big. For instance in August 1648 Father Bressani returned to Huronia from Quebec with a fleet of 60 canoes carrying 250 Hurons and 26 Frenchmen.

Since the mid-1630s, and especially from 1641 on, the Frenchmen and the Huron Indians increasingly had problems with the Iroquois from the south who desperately wanted access to the rich sources of fur controlled by the Hurons. On the Ottawa River the Iroquois also regularly intercepted the Huron fur convoys coming from the French River on their way to Quebec or the fleets going back to Huronia.

This eventually led to all-out war, culminating in the destruction of the villages and missions in Huronia in 1648 and 1649 by the well-armed Iroquois. Great numbers of Hurons were killed as well as several Jesuit priests, among them Brébeuf and Lalemant, who were tortured to death on 16 and 17 March 1649.

In the spring of that year, following the annihilation of their country, the Hurons still remain-ing after the epidemics and the war began to leave their villages, dispersing to different parts of the country in the north, west, and southwest. The Jesuit missionaries and other Frenchmen still alive also fled but first they burned Ste-Marie to the ground on 14 June 1649.

They left for their new mission, an Indian village on Christian Island in Georgian Bay about 3 kilometres off the northwest coast of the Huron peninsula, with at least two thousand and maybe even six thousand or more Hurons, who soon found out that their misery was far from over. Starvation, disease, and Iroquois raiding parties haunted and decimated them during the harsh winter and many Indians died an agonizing death.

Under the leadership of Father Ragueneau, the priests and the other Frenchmen (sixty in all) decided to escape the horrific conditions on Christian Island. They left for Quebec on 10 June 1650 with about three hundred Christian Hurons, carrying with them the hallowed bones of Brébeuf and Lalemant that they had salvaged.

How they travelled is not known; they probably canoed along the Georgian Bay coast to the French River and from there on took the familiar fur-trade route east. Or they could have walked north to the French River or Lake Nipissing and then continued eastward following the Mattawa and Ottawa rivers. The more than three hundred survivors were found near the Ottawa River by Father Bressani, who had left Quebec for Huronia on a rescue mission with about twenty-two canoes, thirty to thirty-five Frenchmen, and thirty Indians. After forty-nine days the refugees finally reached Montreal on 28 July following a very difficult trip that had taken them 850 kilometres (530 miles). With the speed of their travel, which took them an average distance of 17 kilometres (10 miles) per day, it is most likely that the group made at least part of the trip by canoe via the French River trade route.

It must have been a terrible sight, those hundreds of emaciated men, women, and children struggling through the bush and across rivers and lakes, rapids and portages, trying desperately to reach a safe haven many hundreds of kilometres away.

This sad tragedy was the final episode in the four-decade-long enterprise that saw the French River perform a major role as part of the busy highway connecting Huronia with New France. The river played host to a widely varied cast of characters, hurrying across its waters in thousands of canoes, frantically searching for fulfilment of their dreams. The river would gradually begin to welcome other people, other action, other stories. The French River would become an integral part of the developing fur trade to the south, west, and eventually far northwest that would dominate the activities on the river for the next two hundred years.

Snapping turtle.

FUR TRADE

The Huron middlemen had been eliminated by 1650 and new sources of fur had to be found by the Frenchmen in order to keep their trade alive and satisfy the huge European demand for fur. The obvious lands to explore were the vast regions to the west.

Before 1650 a few explorers had travelled west in search of new horizons. The earliest of these was probably Etienne Brûlé, who, in 1621, is said to have travelled northwest from Huronia. He was likely the first white man to see the upper Great Lakes, Huron, Michigan, and Superior.

Another early explorer was Jean Nicollet, who, in 1618, had been sent by Champlain to live with the Algonquin and later the Nipissing Indians and learn from them. In July 1634, Nicollet left New France and went to Lake Nipissing where he recruited an escort of seven Indians, then paddled down the French River to the west. He travelled along the north shore of Georgian Bay into Lake Huron, visited Ste. Marie's Straits as well as Michilimackinac, continued to the west

Ready for another day of exploring; looking southeast across Double Rapids.

coast of Lake Michigan, and finally returned to New France via the French River route in the fall of 1635.

From before the destruction of Huronia until the mid-1650s, Iroquois raids on fur fleets going up and down the Ottawa River made transportation between the west and Quebec very difficult and only occasionally successful. In those years the French River saw little action. What action it did see came from the Ottawa Indians living in the Sault Ste. Marie area and further west, who had taken over part of the middleman role from the Hurons. They assembled fleets loaded with fur obtained from Indian tribes to the west and north of them and tried to take these to Montreal using the French–Ottawa route.

In the 1650s, the French began to reorganize their damaged operations and the fur trade slowly took on a new life. Growing numbers of coureurs de bois, independent white traders, began to play an important role by going into the fur-producing country themselves and dealing directly with the Natives. Instead of waiting for them to come down to the trading places supervised by the French colonial officials, the coureurs de bois, supreme individualists who had abandoned farming for the much more profitable and exciting fur trade and who disdained all authority, began living with the Indians and adapting to their way of life, thus becoming highly skilled woodsmen and canoeists.

Sometimes these coureurs de bois were allowed by the French authorities to trade, but most often they were not and therefore risked being punished severely if they were caught breaking the law. Nevertheless, the profits to be had in the fur trade were so attractive and the lure of a free life so irresistible that many young men from New France ventured into the fur country on their own. By 1680 there were about five hundred coureurs de bois in the Lake Superior area alone.

At the same time, more and more trips to the fur country were being organized by small partnerships of New France merchants, who began to hire men from their own region to paddle the merchants' canoes to and from the interior instead of having Indians bring the fur down to Quebec. Thus were born the voyageurs, paid laborers who would play an increasingly important role in the fur trade and whose physical endurance and mastery of canoeing would power numerous canoe trips on the French River and countless other rivers for another two hundred years.

Between 1654 and 1660, two important canoe trips took place that would radically influence the history of the fur trade and consequently that of Canada. These trips became possible after peace was made with the Iroquois in early 1654, reopening the established Ottawa–French route to the west and once more enabling the western Indians to get to Quebec.

On 6 August 1654, thirty-six-year-old Médard Chouart Des Groseilliers and an unknown French companion, who were in fact coureurs de bois, accompanied a group of these western Ottawa–Huron Indians on a trip authorized by the Governor of New France to expand the fur trade beyond the known western frontiers. Toward the end of August 1656, Des Groseilliers and his partner returned to Quebec from Wisconsin and the southwestern shore of Lake Superior via the French River with 50 fur-filled canoes paddled by 250 Indians. The riches the victorious explorer-trader brought back were received by the French with great joy as they saved the economy of New France from certain ruin.

The newly acquired knowledge about Lake Michigan and Lake Superior would provide great opportunities for fur traders and Jesuit missionaries to expand their respective fields of operation. This was the beginning of the large-scale organized fur trade that would grow to form the basis of the New France economy for many years.

Eager to repeat and possibly improve on his tremendous success in the western fur regions, Des Groseilliers, now accompanied by his brother-in-law, Pierre Esprit Radisson (then twenty-three years old), planned to go west again, in spite of strong objections from the Governor who wanted to exert strict control over the fur trade. They left Trois-Rivières in August 1659 on an unlicensed expedition that would take them to the southwest shore of Lake Superior (now north-western Wisconsin) where they wintered. The following spring they moved on to the lake's north shore.

The partners amassed huge amounts of fur. They arrived in Montreal on 19 August 1660 by way of the French River with a fortune in furs loaded in sixty canoes paddled by three hundred Indians. They returned to Trois-Rivières on 24 August. In spite of producing another tremendous boost to the economy, Radisson and Des Groseilliers were severely punished for having defied the Governor's command. The two were arrested and heavily fined, and their fur was confiscated by the authorities.

The consequences of that unauthorized trip would be far reaching. Radisson and Des Groseilliers wanted to organize the fur trade so that exchange of fur and goods between canoe parties coming from the rich fur regions in the interior (west and northwest of Lake Superior) and European ships from the sea should take place in trading centres on the Hudson Bay coast. They would thus avoid the long, dangerous, and increasingly expensive French–Ottawa fur-trade route to Quebec.

But the people in New France didn't want to listen to these Hudson Bay plans. They were afraid their Quebec-centred fur trade would suffer if the trading activities were moved north. So Radisson and Des Groseilliers tried to find other minds more open to their ideas; eventually they found them in England. There, based on their proposals and after a successful trial expedition, the Hudson's Bay Company was granted a charter on 2 May 1670 for the exclusive rights to establish a trade in fur with the Indians in all the lands drained by Hudson Bay.

Thus began a hard and increasingly vicious fight for control of the fur trade in a large part of northern North America that would last for about 150 years until 1821.

In the second half of the seventeenth century, the Quebec-centred fur trade gradually expanded as its organization improved. In 1681 a system of licenses was set up to give the French authorities more control of the trade and the people involved in it. Although there were continuing problems with the Iroquois who occasionally tried to obstruct the traffic on the Ottawa River, new trade routes were developed that again followed the Ottawa and French Rivers but then went west, southwest, and south to the fur-rich lands of Wisconsin, Minnesota, Michigan, Illinois, and Ohio.

The importance of Michilimackinac, strategically placed in the strait between lakes Huron and Michigan, steadily grew and it became the hub of much trading activity. Detroit, located between lakes Huron and Erie, also developed into an important trading centre. Much of the traffic to and from these regions went via the traditional Ottawa–French route, but some of it also used the shorter route following the St. Lawrence River and lakes Ontario and Erie.

But the French now had competition. The English also wanted a share of the spoils. During the next one hundred years (until 1760) there would be four wars between the French and the English. In spite of English interference, the fur trade along the now well-established Ottawa-French route continued year after year, bringing magnificent fortunes to the merchants of New France as well as opening great opportunities for missionaries to establish missions in new regions.

An important step in the opening-up of the western fur country was a series of expeditions made by Pierre Gaultier de Varenne et de la Vérendrye with three of his sons and a nephew in the 1730s. They were the first explorers to go far to the west of Lake Superior and to see the Prairies as well as the foothills of the Rocky Mountains. La Vérendrye also shipped large quantities of fur to the French merchants in Quebec via the French-Ottawa route. These new finds opened many opportunities for expansion as more and more productive fur areas were discovered.

The French fur trade reached its pinnacle around 1750, but the competition was increasing too and dark clouds were starting to appear on the horizon. The animosity between the French and English finally exploded in 1754 when war broke out in the colonies. The war was lost by the French in 1760 when the English occupied Quebec. This meant the end of New France and the collapse of the 150-year-old French fur trade that had seen innumerable canoes and people go back and forth between the St. Lawrence settlements and the rich fur countries in the rapidly opening-up interior.

Almost all of these travellers had paddled the waters of the French River, walked its portages, and camped on its shores, tracing the legendary fur-trade route to the West, which would remain in existence for another sixty years until 1821 and then continue in a simplified form until the middle of the nineteenth century.

Canadian Shield bedrock at the Pickerel River Outlet.

CHAPTER 4

BRITISH PERIOD (1760—1867)

FUR TRADE

The year was 1760, the Conquest was over, New France had lost the war (the peace treaty would be signed in 1763), and its most important industry was in trouble. For a short while not much was happening on the French River or anywhere else in the French fur country.

But soon new entrepreneurs surfaced in Montreal, all speaking English (Scotsmen and Englishmen from across the ocean and traders from the American colonies to the south) and all eager to invest time, money, and effort to replace the Frenchmen and revive the lucrative trade. The tough, shrewd, and clannish merchants from the Scottish Highlands would play a major role in the fur trade during the next sixty years and also for several decades beyond that.

Initially, the parties in Montreal consisted of a number of small companies and individual merchants, each trying to establish a viable line of communication with the ever expanding fur-producing interior. These multiple efforts inevitably led to a great deal of expensive inefficiency and, during several years of increasingly cutthroat competition, many of the minor players dropped by the wayside. It became obvious that the best solution to the problem of establishing a healthy fur trade would be for several parties to pool their resources and work together closely.

In 1779, one of the Montreal merchants, Simon McTavish, twenty-nine, and several of his fellow traders therefore organized a loose partnership called the North West Company. In 1783 they put the company on a more solid basis by reorganizing it into a unified, formal, and permanent multiple partnership. In the flourishing fur trade, the aggressive NWC, headquartered in Montreal, would quickly become the main rival of the Hudson's Bay Company operating from the shores of Hudson Bay.

With the Conquest, the new Montreal fur traders gained access to the long established and very important fur-producing territory in the southwest Great Lakes region (Michigan, Wisconsin, Illinois, Ohio), which had been developed and exploited by the French for many years, producing a major part of their revenue. But through exciting discoveries by some NWC explorers, the Montrealers soon found out that to the west and especially the northwest of the Great Lakes, immense lands existed that, because of the colder climate and longer winters in those northern latitudes, promised to deliver greater numbers of better quality fur than the south.

Some of those explorers, who regularly paddled the French River on their travels to and from the West, would become household names revered by many for the prosperity they brought to the country. Alexander Henry (the Elder) went west from Montreal on 4 August 1761 and became the first Englishman after the Conquest to paddle the French River and trade on Lake Superior and the areas west of it. He would continue to roam these lands for more than a decade.

Peter Pond started out in 1775 (when he was thirty-five) to help explore the Highway to the West. In 1778 he was the first white man to walk the 21-kilometre (13 miles) Methye Portage which crosses the height of land separating the drainage systems of southern Hudson Bay and the Arctic, connecting the Churchill River system to the Athabasca River via the Clearwater River. His discovery of this important portage opened the road to the enormous country around Lake Athabasca, 4,000 kilometres (2,500 miles) from Montreal by canoe, a strange and fascinating land filled with the most luxurious and profitable furs to be found anywhere.

Alexander Mackenzie would become one of the leading partners in the North West Company. In 1789 at the age of twenty-five, he became the first white man to travel the Mackenzie River and reach the Polar Sea. He was also the first, in 1793, to cross the northern latitudes of North America to the Pacific Ocean by canoe. In those four years Mackenzie had travelled 16,000 kilometres (10,000 miles).

The NWC did not hesitate to follow these pioneers into the new lands in their quest for more and better furs, but the merchants soon found out they required an efficient way to stay in contact with Montreal in order to remain in business. The steadily growing fur-producing interior was now becoming so vast and the canoe routes were getting so long that it was impossible to get the fur to the Montreal warehouses from the farthest reaches of the interior in one canoeing season (May to October) and still have time enough to return to base camp.

A system was therefore developed whereby the trunk route between Montreal and Fort Chipewyan on Lake Athabasca was split into two sections. Each section was travelled by the kind of birchbark canoe best suited to it. Very big freight canoes, canots du maître, were used on the section between Montreal and the NWC's inland headquarters at the northwest end of Lake Superior — a trip that could take up to two months. Until 1803 this headquarters was at Grand Portage and after that at Fort Kamanistiquia, which was renamed Fort William in 1807. There the freight was transferred to smaller canoes, canots du nord, which were paddled on the second section to Fort Chipewyan and the other trading posts located on the trunk line and the secondary branch lines.

The canot du maître, or Montreal canoe, was on average 11 metres (36 feet) long with a maximum width of 1.5 metres (5 feet) and depth of 0.9 metres (3 feet). It had an empty weight of 230 kilograms (500 pounds), a carrying capacity of about 3,500 kilograms (7,700 pounds), and was usually paddled by eight to twelve men, who could give the craft a speed of 7–9 kilometres per hour (4.4–5.6 miles per hour) in windless conditions on flatwater. The length, which could vary between 9.8 and 12.2 metres (32–40 feet), gave the craft great efficiency: it was fast, could be used on lakes, and had sufficient freeboard to be paddled in considerable waves.

A special type of Montreal canoe was the light or express canoe, usually between 9.8 and 10.4 metres (32–34 feet) long, used between Montreal and the inland headquarters to transport people, urgent mail and dispatches, and special goods as quickly as possible. These relatively light-loaded canoes were often manned by fourteen or more top-quality paddlers, who could give it a tremendous speed of at least 10 kilometres per hour (6.3 miles per hour), enabling the party to reach their destination in record time. Under the right circumstances an express canoe could travel a distance of 140 kilometres in eighteen hours of hard paddling.

The famous paintings created by Frances Anne Hopkins are based on observations made during her trips of the 1860s and give an authentic indication of what Montreal and express canoes looked like. (See pages 99, 100, 106, and 110.)

The men powering these huge but graceful Montreal canoes were the famous voyageurs. Most of them were French-Canadians, but there were also Indians, Blacks, and Scotsmen. The voyageurs were capable of spending up to eighteen hours per day paddling, portaging, lining, and poling their craft and cargo across great distances. They were paid laborers, part of a system inherited from the previous French period; most of them were recruited from the townships around Montreal, Trois-Rivières, and Quebec City. Even through the times of the NWC the French language of the voyageurs dominated canoeing. Today words like voyageur, avant, milieu, bourgeois, gouvernail, portage, and décharge are still commonly used in English canoeing circles. There are also many celebrated voyageur songs in French.

The canot du nord, or North canoe, paddled in the vast country west and northwest of Lake Superior, had a length varying between 6.7 and 7.9 metres (22 and 26 feet). A 7.6-metre (25 feet) canoe typically weighed 140 kilograms (300 pounds) and could carry 1,400 kilograms (3,000 pounds). It was powered by four or more extra-tough elite voyageurs who would winter inland and often would not return to Montreal for several years.

Using this system of specialized canoes paddled by experienced and powerful voyageurs, the Montreal fur trade flourished for several decades (between 1779 and 1821, the period of the Montreal–Athabasca fur-trade route). Although the best-known company in Montreal during those years was the NWC, other trading associations as well as independent traders, and sometimes even the NWC's powerful rival, the Hudson's Bay Company, used Montreal as a starting point for trips inland following the established Ottawa–French route.

In the spring, several NWC brigades, each ranging from a few Montreal freight canoes to more than ten, and filled to overflowing with goods, equipment, and people, would go down the French River to Georgian Bay, trying to get as quickly as possible to the company's inland headquarters, the main trans-shipment point on the northwest coast of Lake Superior.

Besides the standard trade goods such as pots, pails, kettles, knives, axes, guns, lead shot and balls, canisters of gunpowder, pieces of iron and other metals, traps, hats, blankets, handkerchiefs, pieces of cloth; and special trade goods such as small brooches, earrings, crosses, medals, large pieces of silver, armbands, headbands, gorgets, ear ornaments, wristbands, and bracelets, the big canoes also carried many other articles. The following items would often be stored in wooden kegs small enough to be portaged: tobacco, hams, grease, sweets, white and brown sugar, salt, brandy, rum, spirits, port wine, red wine, Madeira wine, vinegar, pork, beef, fish, butter, tongue, sausages, flour, rice, corn, peas, spices, cheese, raisins, figs, prunes, food for the paddling crew (peas, pork, biscuits, rum), and soap. They would also carry items for making camp and repairing canoes including cooking pots, crooked knives, rope, axes, tin plates, rolls of birchbark, spruce gum, and spruce roots; mirrors, musical instruments such as bagpipes and fiddles; a sail, oil cloths, and sponge. They sometimes carried special items such as candelabras and candles, cutlery, plates, wine decanters, fine wine glasses, tea cups, finger bowls, English crystal, Chinese porcelain, earthenware, creamware (also called queensware), table cloths, napkins, Irish linen, and other luxury articles requested by the gentlemen in Fort William.

Late in the eighteenth century, sailing schooners were beginning to operate between ports in southern Lake Huron and Sault Ste. Marie, and on Lake Superior, taking over some of the transportation of heavy and bulky items including large kegs with high wine and other provisions, cattle, horses, swine, anvils, and even cannons. Using these ships was cheaper but also slower than moving everything by canoe via the French River.

Little French Dam and Hall Chute, looking north.

In August or September, the Montreal freight canoes would be hauled back up the French River loaded with fortunes in fur. Although beaver was by far the most important kind of fur traded, many other species were also in demand such as fox, wolf, muskrat, otter, marten, mink, fisher, black and grizzly bear, lynx, deer, raccoon, buffalo, moose, wolverine, and even swan and goose skins. The amount of fur handled during the trade's heyday was staggering. In 1806, for instance, 77,500 beaver pelts were recorded in the fur warehouse of Fort Kamanistiquia, which translates into about 50 tons of beaver skins for that one year alone.

The big canoes often carried NWC officials and personnel (agents and clerks) to and from the annual rendez-vous in the interior headquarters where important company matters were discussed. The wives and children of the men living in the interior were occasional passengers as were sick people and prisoners. Independent fur traders would also travel to Montreal and back via the French River. One famous explorer who once travelled on the French River was David Thompson, a surveyor–cartographer–geographer who, in 1812, after twenty-eight years in the interior, returned to his home in the province of Quebec accompanied by his wife and family.

An impressive example of the blazing speed possible by express canoes is the trip made by Simon McGillivray, agent-shareholder of the North West Company, who travelled from Montreal down the French River on his way to an annual rendezvous and business meeting in Fort William, 1,500 kilometres (940 miles) away. He started in Montreal on 21 June 1815 and arrived in Fort William on 9 July, a total of only eighteen days (normally a freight brigade would need six to eight weeks for this trip). McGillivray returned to Montreal two weeks later, again via the French River, and this time made it in three weeks (25 July–17 August). This was the first canoe trip the hardy Scot had ever made.

These were fascinating and profitable times for the fur traders. During most of the years between 1779 and 1821 the French River was a busy highway indeed. Those four decades, especially the years around 1815, made up the glory times of the NWC. These years also included the War of 1812 and other armed conflicts near and far such as the American and French Revolutions and the Napoleonic Wars and the resulting sea-route blockades. But the biggest problem the NWC encountered, underfinanced and suffering from long and expensive canoe routes across the whole continent, was the increasingly bitter fight with the HBC for effective control of the fur trade.

The trouble between the companies escalated until, in 1821, the HBC and the NWC wisely decided to amalgamate under the name of the former. From this time on there would be few freight canoes on the main route from Montreal to the interior as almost all transportation of goods, fur, and people would take place by boat directly between the HBC posts on the shores of Hudson Bay and the inland posts.

But the Ottawa–French route was not dead; it would continue to see some canoeing activity connected to the fur trade for another forty years or so. The French River was still being travelled occasionally by canoes, often the large express canoes. George Simpson, who was governor of the Hudson's Bay Company for thirty-nine years, from 1821 to 1860, made it a point to visit the interior posts as often as possible from his headquarters in Montreal and was thus a frequent visitor to the French River. Between 1820 and 1859, he made the canoe trip to the west about twenty-seven times in an express canoe powered by fourteen specially selected voyageurs, often Iroquois Indians, and usually accompanied by his Scottish piper.

This specialized canoe traffic eventually petered out too with a deepening depression in the fur trade. Fashion was changing in Europe; starting in the 1840s, cheaper lacquered silk was slowly taking over from beaver felt as the preferred material for fashionable hats. By the 1860s, the three-hundred-year-old dictatorial rule of the beaver hat was finally over; there were to be no more birchbark canoes on the French River racing to the interior in a mad hunt for huge fortunes.

During those three hundred years, unimaginable numbers of animals had been slaughtered to satisfy the insatiable demands of the European fashion industry. The beaver had been trapped almost to extinction. It is estimated that early in the sixteenth century North America had a beaver population of about thirty million; by the middle of the nineteenth century there was only a fraction of this left. Astounding numbers of pelts had been transported across North America's rivers and lakes, many millions of them carried up the French River in a fantastic procession of thousands of birchbark canoes. The beaver has since returned in most places and the population is again thriving.

A great old era was ending and a new one was about to begin, moving the river to a modern life based on resource extraction, settlement, and tourism.

TRAVELLERS' TALES
Of the countless travellers that the French River has seen over the years, a few kept diaries or journals describing, often in broad strokes but sometimes in considerable detail, what they observed while on the river.

Dalles Rapids, looking east.

These narratives were not always shining examples of accurate and objective reporting; the writers sometimes resorted to copying each other, repeating mistakes, giving varying interpretations, and occasionally jumping back and forth between locations. But many of the stories still make fascinating reading because of the first-hand information they offer about canoe tripping through a rugged, unknown wilderness.

A few of the more interesting narratives are presented below, sometimes slightly edited and shortened for modern readers. No effort has been made to correlate place names in the journals with contemporary ones; there are quite a few discrepancies that often make it difficult to know the exact routes followed by these early travellers on the French River.

The first-hand accounts of Alexander Henry (the Elder) appear in his book, *Travels and Adventures in Canada and the Indian Territories Between the Years 1760 and 1776*, published in 1809. He had this to say about the French River:

> The carrying-place of La Chaudière Française is at the head of the River des Français, and where the water first descends from the level of Lake Nipisingue toward that of Lake Huron. This it does not reach till it has passed down many rapids, full of danger to the canoes and the men, after which it enters Lake Huron by several arms, flowing through each as through mill-race. The River des Français is twenty leagues in length and has many islands in its channel. Its banks are uniformly of rock. Among the carrying-places at which we successively arrived are the Portage des Pins, or du Pin; de la Grande Faucille; de la Petite Faucille; and du Sault du Recolet. Near the mouth of the river a meadow, called La Prairie des Français, varies for a short space the rocky surface which so generally prevails; and on this spot we encamped and repaired our canoes. The carrying-places were now all passed, and what remained was to cross the billows of Lake Huron, which lay stretched across our horizon like an ocean.
>
> On the thirty-first day of August we entered the lake, the waves running high from the south, and breaking over numerous rocks.

Alexander Mackenzie was a fur trader and explorer who became a partner in the North West Company in 1787 and travelled the French River several times on his way to and from the rich interior fur country. In his book, *Voyages from Montreal*, first published in 1801 and one of the classics of the fur-trade literature, he presented the following information about the river:

> Out of it [Lake Nipissing] flows the Riviere des François, over rocks of a considerable height. In a bay to the east of this, the road leads over the Portage of the Chaudiere des François, five hundred and

forty-four paces, to still water. It must have acquired the name of Kettle, from a great number of holes in the solid rock of a cylindrical form, and not unlike that culinary utensil. .... The French river is very irregular, both as to its breadth and form, and is so interspersed with islands, that in the whole course of it the banks are seldom visible. Of its various channels, that which is generally followed by the canoes is obstructed by the following Portages, viz., des Pins, fifty-two paces; Feausille, thirty-six paces; Parisienne, one hundred paces; Recolet, forty-five paces; and the Petite Feusille, twenty-five paces. In several parts there are guts or channels, where the water flows with great velocity, which are not more than twice the breadth of a canoe. The distance of Lake Huron is estimated at twenty-five leagues, which this river enters in the latitude 45.53. North, that is, at the point of land three or four miles within the lake. There is hardly a foot of soil to be seen from one end of the French river to the other, its banks consisting of hills of entire rock.

John Macdonnell was a young clerk of the North West Company who, in 1793, made his first canoe trip into the interior. His following account is given in "The Diary of John Macdonnell" in *Five Fur Traders of the Northwest*, edited by Charles M. Gates and published in reprint edition 1965 by the Minnesota Historical Society.

At the chaudiere des Français we carry from the Lake nipising to a deep still water cove of the River des Français, which issues out of the Lake by a variety of channels to the North North West of the portage and are too rapidious to be navigable above if they are to be judged of by [the] nearest of them to the portage which is steeper than a mill race and not wider in places. After proceeding about two miles down the cove [where] we carried from Lac Nipising the current of the main body of the Français River comming from the N.N.E. took us broad side and carried us down merrily being the first current able to make an impression on the canoe that we have drifted with. At the Chaudiere des Français I saw the first Juniper berry growing but now they are to be met with all along the French River.

June 26th Came down the following Rapids, Les Pins, Rapide Croche, La Fausille, Le Parisien, petit parisien. The day is a beautiful clear day and sun shine. Have seen nothing but rocks since we entered the French River producing moss and some ever-greens stinted in growth, one would think that a bird could scarcely live on these Rocks.

Fourteen leagues from Lake Nipising is L'Enfant perdu a fine encampment .... A league below l'Enfant perdue under the high rocky ground and wood back of their encampment is a portage called le Grand Recolet where one of the North West Companys canoes manned by brothers of the name of Majeau [upset] and lost half the cargo about fifteen days ago. The few survivors and the goods that floated were picked [up] below the Rapid by the other canoes of the Brigade. These unfortunate men had made portage and loaded their canoe below it, but had neglected to put a men or two on shore with a bit of Line to stem the strong eddy which carries back to fall, from a foolish confidence in their own power, and in consequence were drawn down by the eddy under the pitch of the fall where the canoe instantly filled and sunk. Though some of the bodies were found far below this the seven crosses are erected here as a warning to others along with seven others in memory of former casualties. Two leagues below the Grand Recollet is Derraud's Rapid named after a voyageur of that name who broke his Canoe in it; this being the communication between Lake Huron and the ottawa River appears to have been much frequented by the savages of old, as may be judged from the various figures of animals &c. made by them on the face of the steep Rocks in many places along the banks. Some leagues below Derreaud's Rapid is the figure of a man standing over an animal that lays under him .... Two leagues from Lake Huron there is a figure of an ox which gives name to a fine long View of the river called Lad du Boeuf.

 After passing a narrow Racy rapid named the Dalles we saw an Island on which as the story goes, the Irroquois in former days, say 40 or 50 Years ago tried to cut off a strong Brigade of trading canoes....

 Thursday June 27th. After coming 25 Leagues yesterday and today, which is, the full length of the French River, from Lake Nipising to lake Huron, we entered the latter with a very strong headwind....

Angus Mackintosh was a North West Company agent who, in 1813, made a trip from Michili-mackinac to Montreal going *up* the French River. The following is an excerpt from his extensive diary which he titled *Journal from the Enterance of the French River to Montreal in a Cannoe from Michilimackinac in Company with Mr. Henry Parker, left Michilimackinac on the forenoon of thursday the 8th July 1813* (a copy is available in the Archives of Ontario under: Diary, Mackintosh Papers, MU 1956).

 13th Entered the French River on the evening of this day, soon after encamped for the night.

 14th This morning left our encamping ground and proceeded up the river, came to the Dalle a rapid of 50 feet of very strong water where the cannoe was dragged up by the line (5 codelines twisted together). Soon after getting up this rapids we came to Le Petit Faucille a rapid and carrying place of 60 feet.... Next is the strong waters of Le Denneaux; arrived at the L'Enfant Perdu and encamped here, and a favourable situation for encamping; back from the river is very high rocks.

 15th This morning, rained until midday. When we left L'Enfant Perdu proceeded up a narrow strait, course of East by North, twenty miles, which brought us to the les Petites Parisian, or the Parisian

Croche about 120 feet long, here the river winds much - and about twelve feet wide, and used the codelines to drag. About half a mile distance is the Portage Parisian, here the river is divided by an island where we encamped for the night. Cannoes half loaded go down on the North side and are hauled up on the South, and the carrying place across the rocks about 120 feet.

16th Left the Parisian this morning at midday from bad weather. The next portage is the Grand Faucille 120 feet across the carrying place; next you come to the Rapid Croche, but do not unload. Soon after we got to the Grand Batture, and proceeded on until we came to the Rapid au Pin, where we carried up a rock 30 feet high. The carrying place is about 150 feet over. At 7 P.M. arrived at and encamped at the Chaudiere des Francois, at this place we had a fine ham stolen out of my basket and it could not be discovered who committed the act.

17th This morning, commenced sending the cannoes and packs to the other end of the carrying place, and soon after the whole was got over a heavy rain came on. Pitched our tent, got our tea kettle boiled and breakfasted, tho before we had well done, the rain water was running under our baggage in the tent, that we were obliged to strick the tent and remove it to a flat part of a rocks near to where we first were. The rain subsiding at 10 A.M. we left this encampment and came on 15 miles when we arrived at the west end of Lake Nippinsang, when the wind blew so violent that we were degraded until 4 P.M. when we recommensed our journey tho still in heavy swell. We however got on about 9 miles when it began to get dark and we encamped in a fine bay, surrounded with large pine trees.

Jean Baptiste Perrault travelled extensively while working in the fur trade as a merchant for several companies and also doing some other work. Originally written in about 1830 in French (and translated into English around 1905) from diaries probably kept by Perrault, the journal tells a detailed story of his many voyages. The following is adapted from both French and English editions and relates his trip down the French River in early June 1815 when he was about fifty-four.

... we camped at the Portage de la Chaudière des François, so-called because of three cauldrons made by the art of nature, which resemble vats or cauldrons for potash as perfectly as if made by the hand of man. The portage is three to four arpents in length, over living rock; at the end of which, one takes the Rivière des François, which is reckoned 25 leagues to its emptying place, Lake Huron.

The first rapid one has to shoot is that of L'Isle aux Pins; the second, that of Les Grandes Faucilles; the third, the Rapide de Parisien, where one makes a portage at high water, because here a man named Parisien and several others were drowned; the fourth is Le Grand Récollet, or Le Petit Récollet,

Eastern Outlet, looking east.

which are separated one from another by an island about a league long. Going up from there, one comes to Les Dalles so called because the river contracts itself at that place to the width of forty to sixty feet for about four or five arpents, of which one side is a rock sheer and smooth, and tilted to an angle of nearly 45 degrees, so that when the water is very high those who attempt to tow their boats by a line have a great deal of trouble to ascend. The other bank just across is quite high and strewn with broken rocks of all sizes, where the Yroquois used to lie in ambush to attack the French who came to trade at that time on Lake Huron. For it appears that the Hurons as well as the Yroquois of those days would come to carry on their forays even to Lakes Huron and Superior, seeing that they were defeated by the Sauteux, who had discovered them at the point which bears the name of Pointe aux Yroquois to this day....

Below Le Récollet, there is a shallow rapid which is short. Here I was delayed, I myself, together with the ten men in the canoe, being compelled to take to the water, in order to get by that place. From that place one encounters Les Petites Faucilles, where one unloads and reloads immediately, and the boat shoots about twice its length in the form of a sickle. From there one can, by going a couple of leagues, gain the lakes.

Robert Seaborne Miles was the twenty-two-year-old secretary of Colin Robertson of the Hudson's Bay Company who returned to Fort Wedderburn on Lake Athabaska in 1818. Miles' extensive records of the canoe trip from Lachine to the northwest verify that the HBC also used the French River route for some of their trips from Montreal to the interior. Their party consisted of four white men in two North canoes (instead of the one customary express canoe) manned by Iroquois Indians and one black man.

As was usually the case with these express trips, the group travelled fast. They left Lachine on 28 May, entered the French River on 7 June at about 7 A.M. and Georgian Bay on 8 June at 1 P.M., reached Sault St. Marie on 11 June, and entered the Kamanistiquia River (passing Fort William, which belonged to the competing North West Company) on 24 June. The following is an excerpt from his journals (a copy is available in the Archives of Ontario under: Box 7-10, MU 1391).

FRENCH RIVER, Sunday 7th June 1818.

Embarked this morning at half past two o'clock. I had the pleasure of enjoying good repose last night for the first time since we first embarked, not having any moschito's to torment us, which had been the case at every other encampment. Quarter past seven entered the French River, and in fifteen minutes put ashore to breakfast, left again in an hour. Twenty minutes to eleven reached Portage Chaudiere de

Francois, carried the bagage and gummed the canoe and left at twenty-five minutes to twelve. Fifteen minutes to two put ashore to dine, here one of our men was so much indisposed that Mr. R. came under the necessity of giving him a flannel dress, this detained us 'till half past three. Encamped at seven o'clock at a place called by the Indians 'the lost child,' this takes its name from the circumstance of a child's being lost which they were never able to trace.

LAKE HEURON , Monday 8th June 1818.

Left our encampment this morning at half past four o'clock, and in twenty minutes came up with a small band of Indians who on our passing gave us a volley of firearms, out of respect to Mr. Robertson whom they learnt from Mr. McLeod's brigade that passed there yesterday morning, was expected hourly. The Indians followed us to the Recollet Portage where we arrived at half past five. They presented Mr. R. with a skin and some maple sugar, for which he gave them a small keg of mix't rum and a little biscuit. Left again at six and proceeded until seven o'clock when we put ashore to breakfast and embarked again in an hour. Fifteen minutes to nine entered Lake Buffaloe and at a quarter past eleven entered the Dalles. These are a number of narrow gut ways through rocks, from which the French River empties itself into Lake Heuron. At one o'clock p.m. entered the lake and immediately traversed a few small bays.

John J. Bigsby was a British army surgeon and geologist who travelled the French River in 1819 during a tour of Upper and Lower Canada to investigate geological resources. His two-volume book, *The Shoe and Canoe*, was published in 1850 and presents a wealth of information on the conditions in the country as he saw them during his travels. The following is an excerpt from that book.

We leave Lake Nipissing by the Portage Chaudière des François. It is near the falls of the same name, and leads over low ridges of naked gneis, and here and there a cliff, to a backwater of the interesting River des François, by which this lake discharges into Lake Huron.

The falls are principally to be noticed for several smooth, funnel-shaped holes in the solid rock, near the lake, but twenty feet above its present level. One is from three to four feet deep, and as many across at the top, but only eighteen inches at the bottom.

They are supposed to be caused by the friction of stones whirled round by an eddy, as they have actually been seen where eddies have been known to exist. The other holes (or kettles) are smaller, as far as I recollect....

Cross Channel Rapids at low water.

I shall not dwell long on the River des François, which we descended fast and gaily, lest I become tedious, although it is a very peculiar river. It less resembles a single stream than a bundle of watercourses flowing, with frequent inosculations, among lengthened ridges of rocks. The utterly barren and naked shores seldom present continuous lines bounding a compact body of water, but are commonly excavated into deepened narrow bays, obscured by high walls of rock and stunted pines. It is seventy-five miles long. Its breadth is exceedingly various, sometimes swelling into a broad lake for miles, and crowded with islands....

Beside the Chaudière Cascade there is another called Des Recollets, twenty miles down the river. It is from fifteen to twenty feet high, but narrow, and divided into three portions by two fragments of rock. It is very beautiful in its white waters and dark walls, bristling with dead and living pine, almost naked heights being close at hand.

I was much interested by the ruins of an Indian fort, or look-out, which still remains on a point of land commanding a good view downwards, and, I think, upwards. It was a circular building, about five feet in diameter. When I saw it it was only four and a half feet high. It was carefully constructed of the stones at hand, and would contain a couple of Indian watchers in the days when war seldom ceased....

Indian drawings occur on the smooth face of a gneis mound not far from hence. They are rude sketches of animals and men in various attitudes.

Many rapids occur, but the most serious is that of Brisson. It is very swift and turbulent. As our canoe turned round and round in it, in spite of all our men could do, the sight of thirteen wooden crosses lining the shore, in memory of as many watery deaths, conveyed no more comfort to my mind than do the impaled bodies on the highways of Turkey to the feelings of their surviving robber-friends. The current is always strong, so that we swept down the river in one day.

In descending there is but one portage, that of the Recollet, and it is said, though I cannot believe it, that Indians have dashed over that fall. In ascending there are many portages.

At the upper part of the River des François the neighbouring country attains a moderate height, either in great piles of dislocated rocks or in stair-like ridges. Nearer Lake Huron its environs are lower; and as far as is visible from the canoe, there are destitute of vegetation.

This river discharges itself into Lake Huron in narrow channels formed by parallel, smooth, naked mounds of gneis, a few yards broad, a few feet high, and broken into lengths of twenty to two hundred yards. La Dalle, from three to five miles from Lake Huron, a rapid of uncommon swiftness, is a gut of this kind. It is not more than ten or twelve feet wide, and an hundred yards long. Our canoe flashed through it almost in a moment. Either of its sides I could have touched with a walking-stick.

Nicholas Garry was a future Deputy–Governor (1822–1835) of the Hudson's Bay Company who made his first canoe trip from Lachine to the interior in 1821. The following excerpt from the *Diary of Nicholas Garry*, published in the Proceedings and Transactions of the Royal Society of Canada, second series-volume VI, meeting of May 1900, describes his experiences during the trip on the French River:

Wednesday the 20th June.... We now entered the Rivière des François and came to the Portage, La Chaudière des François, so called from the Number of Small Holes in the Rocks having the Appearance of a Kettle. The River des François is about 75 miles in Length and has more the Appearance of a Lake, forming an innumerable Number of low rocky Islands, so that you never see the Banks. At 8 o'clock we came to the Rapid des Pins. Hitherto we had always ascended the Rapids which is less dangerous both in Appearance and in Reality. Now we had to descend and were broken in by rather a terrific one. The Guide stands on the Gunwale at the Bow to ascertain the Course of the Rapid, he then stands in the Canoe and directs the Steersman how to Shape his Course. The Rapidity with which you descend is wonderful and, I should say, certainly at the Rate of 15 or 20 miles an Hour. To every Rapid is attached a melancholy History of Canoes lost and the Crosses or Burial Places you meet with everywhere prove that they are but too true. It was now nearly dark when we came to the Rapid of the Parisienne which we likewise descended and encamped on a small island at the Foot.

Thursday the 21st June. After passing a restless Night from the Attacks of the Musquitoes and black Fly we embarked at half-past two, — beautiful moonlight. At 7 we came to the Portage of the Recolet where the Canoe is only transported a few Paces to avoid the dangerous Part of the Rapid. A Canoe with 11 men was lost at this Rapid a few years since. The Crosses are still standing on the spot where they were buried. The River continues to run through rocky Islands.

Perhaps the worst Part of Canoe travelling is the Want of Comfort, which attends your Encampment at Night. In most Difficulties and Privations in Life there is always a something which is pleasurable to look forward to, when Comfort and Ease will refresh you and give Relief to your Sufferings. Here the Approach of Night and in other Cases of Rest is rather a matter of Dread than of Desire. The Night is passed under the Sufferings of Bites and Stings, and if at last, worn out, Sleep should close the Eyes the call to embark now awakens you to the renewed Attacks of a Host of bloodthirsty and insatiable Enemies; a Digression occasioned by the Bite of Musquitoes, Sand Flies, Spiders, &c., &c.

At 9 we breakfasted, and at 1/2 past we embarked. After paddling for two Hours we came to a narrow Channel forming a Rapid, and the Banks of high Rocks on each Side so confined as scarcely to

Pl.1 Playing in the fabulous waves of Blue Chute.

*Pl.2 Freeflowing Channel
in the Little French River,
looking northeast.*

*Pl.3 Wolseley Bay,
looking northwest.*

Pl.4 Looking down from the Highway 69 bridge into the Main Channel.

Pl.5 Upper French River

Pl.6 Quiet moments, upstream of Blue Chute.

Pl.7 Narrows at the western end of Five Finger Rapids, looking southwest.

Pl.8 Paddling down the upper Crooked Rapids in the Western Outlets.

Pl.9 Blue Chute and The Gully (left) at low water, looking east.

Pl.10 Upstream view of the Lower Chaudière Rapids at low water, with the Upper Chaudière Rapids in the background.

Pl.11 Montreal canoe being lined down Herring Chute in the Western Outlets at low water.

Pl.12 North canoe in Blue Chute.

*Pl.13 Montreal canoe
caressed by the
evening sun.*

Pl.14 Pickerel River Outlet meets the north-going arm of Georgian Bay, looking west.

Pl.15 Montreal canoe in the East Channel of the Rock Circus at low water, Old Voyageur Channel, Western Outlets, looking northeast.

Pl.16 East Channel of the Pickerel River Outlet below the second short portage at low water, looking north.

Pl.17 Herring Chute, looking south.

Pl.18 Looking for artifacts below The Ladder at very low water.

Pl.19 Colorful mushrooms decorate the forest floor.

Pl.20 Bunchberries

Pl.21 Young moose

Pl.22 Mayfly resting on a fern.

Pl.23 The last paddle of the day.

allow the Canoe to pass; it had the Appearance of a Canal cut in the Rock. After it [we] came to a short carrying Place but the Water being high the Canoe was towed. At 2 o'clock Lake Huron opened upon us with the Appearance of a vast Ocean.

Frances Ramsay Simpson was the eighteen-year-old bride of George Simpson, the Governor of the Hudson's Bay Company who frequently travelled the French River route by express canoe to visit the HBC's many trading places in the interior. His trips were always accomplished at great speed and in relative comfort. This one was the first such adventure for the inexperienced but thrilled young woman who came fresh from the prim and proper Society salons of England to the Canadian wilderness. Mrs. Simpson and her travelling companion, Mrs. McTavish, were the first British women to travel by canoe from Montreal to the heart of the fur country. The following is part of Mrs. Simpson's narrative of this 1830 trip and includes her notes made at the start of the voyage as well as notes made while travelling down the French River, which took the party only about one day. It is reproduced here courtesy *The Beaver*, Dec. 1953 and March 1954.

May 2nd Left La Chine at 4 A.M. in two Canoes, manned by 15 hands each, all strong active, fine looking Canadians. The passengers consisting of Mr. and Mrs. McTavish, & Maid Servant in the one, & Mr. Simpson Myself & Servant in the other accompanied by Messrs. Keith & Gale who kindly volunteered to favor us with their company for a day or two.

Our Canoe, a most beautiful craft, airy and elegant beyond description, was 35 feet in length, the lading consisting of 2 Water proof Trunks (known by the name of Cassets) containing our clothes; 1 Basket for holding Cold Meat, Knives & Forks, Towels &c. 1 Egg Basket, a travelling Case (or Canteen) containing 6 Wine Bottles, Cups & Saucers, Tea Pot, Sugar Basin, Spoons, Cruets, Glasses & Tumblers, Fishing Apparatus, Tea, Sugar Salt &c. &c. — also a bag of Biscuits, a bale of Hams, a Keg of Butter &c. &c.

The provisions for the Crew were Pork & Biscuits: from which circumstance the young recruits are called "Pork Eaters" to distinguish them from the old Winterers, who feed chiefly on "Pemican," a mixture of Buffalo Meat, Tallow, and a due proportion of hairs (but wether the last ingredient is intended to keep the composition together or not, I cannot say) this is not the most delicate, but it is very substantial food, and more portable than any other, as it is closely packed in a bag made of Buffalo hide. There is also a keg of liquor (called the Dutchman) from which the people are drammed three or four times a day, according to the state of the Weather.

In this order we started, the voyageurs singing, and the Canoe almost flying thro' the water —

Blue Chute, looking west.

the motion is perfectly easy, & in fine weather it is the most delightful mode of travelling that can be imagined.

10th ... we descended a small river, passed thro' Lake Nipisang, about 40 miles in length, then made a Portage, into the French River. Continued our route thro this river —which is a fine large stream, widening at times, so as to assume the appearance of a Lake: & in some places embanked by high rugged rocks, on the bare faces of which, stunted Pines bristle up deriving their only nourishment from Moss, and held by their long creeping roots, which fasten in the fissures and chasms of these mountains of Granite. Encamped at 7 P.M. — the evening close, with appearance of rain: and I felt rather uncomfortable from an apprehension that we should be visited during the night, by some of the Snakes, with which this place is infested.

11th At the Recollet Portage breakfasted, and the weather clearing up, changed our wet for dry clothes, but on going from the root of the Recollet Fall, were very nearly drawn under it, by a strong Eddy: indeed so near, that the Spray from the fall showered over, & gave us another drenching; but by the exertions of the men at the paddle, regained the Stream, and got into Lake Huron at 2 O'clock.

Upper French River, looking west across Hunt Island.

CHAPTER 5

Canadian Period (from 1867)

By the time the Dominion of Canada was created in 1867, the French River had become a quiet waterway with only an occasional Native fisherman paddling his canoe on the otherwise-deserted waters. The fur-trade times that had lasted on the river for about 250 years and had seen so many birchbark canoes travel its sometimes crowded waters were finally over. From now on, the French River was no longer just a transportation corridor visited only by hurried passers-by; it would instead become home to many newcomers.

Beginning in the 1870s, non-Native Canadians settled in the area to try and make a living from the riches in and around the river's waters, gradually bringing it into a modern world far removed from the fur-trade past. The first settlement of importance was established in the Delta in the mid-1870s once it became clear that the large stands of virgin lumber on the shores of the French River and some of its tributaries were worth harvesting thanks to their easy accessibility from Georgian Bay.

Because of the need for a conveniently located lumbering centre, a townsite called Coponaning was surveyed in 1875 at the Main Outlet of the river, just below Dalles Rapids and enclosing MacDougal Bay, which lies at the end of a 3-kilometre-long (2 miles) north-northeast arm of Georgian Bay (an area that had seen much activity in the fur-trade days and is frequently visited by modern recreational canoeists). Coponaning was also intended as a major terminal for rail and ship transportation. The town would only exist on paper, it was never actually built (see Map 15). Instead, around 1875, when lumber companies were starting small-scale operations in the area, a settlement called French River Village was beginning to grow just south of the Coponaning site, eventually becoming the processing centre for much of the lumbering activities in the French River region. In 1875 a post office was opened here; however, it closed again in the same year.

In the late 1870s, the logging activities were still limited, but then they began to take off in the early 1880s. The big lumber companies had constructed their sawmills and plant buildings at French River Village. The mill town also attracted enough other settlers and businesses that, in

1885, a new post office could be opened that would remain in service until 1922.

The next two decades were the most productive years in the French River logging industry. Several lumber companies were active and French River Village had become a busy centre consisting of two sawmills, two churches, two schools, three hotels, warehouses, houses, offices, stores, and all the other elements of infrastructure required by the hardworking inhabitants who, in 1892, numbered about three hundred.

The raw material used by the mills came from the whole French River area (Voyageur Channel to Lake Nipissing), as well as the Pickerel and Wanapitei Rivers. French River Village was a lively settlement that also saw much traffic by sailboat and steamship to many ports in Ontario and the United States.

In about 1907, a narrow-gauge tramway was constructed south of Dalles Rapids (roughly following the still existing fur-trade portage trail connecting Boiler Point Bay to Dalles Pool) to transport all the material for the Canadian Pacific Railway bridge being built over the French River, 1 kilometre downstream from Dry Pine Bay. The logging companies used this tramway for a while to transport supplies but in the long run it did not meet their demands and was subsequently abandoned.

By 1910 the lumbering business in this area was declining as most of the saleable trees had been cut, sawdust pollution had become a problem for the Georgian Bay fisheries, and the transportation of logs was increasingly being taken over by the railways.

Between 1912 and 1914, the big lumber companies abandoned French River Village and only some smaller operators and a few individuals remained. In 1914 most of the buildings in the settlement were dismantled and shipped out for resale, in 1922 the post office closed for good, and in 1934 the last person still living in the village left the area.

French River Village has become a ghost town. The only structure left standing from the old logging days is the lighthouse, which can still be seen surrounded by some of the ruins of the old buildings, boilers, tanks, and other machinery. In various locations upriver, a few signs of the logging past can still be found — chains, nails, boilers, cables — even the wrecks of two alligator warping tugs lying close to shore upstream of Dalles Rapids, visible when the water is low.

While all these lumbering activities took place in the remote Delta, other developments were happening upriver in the French River area that were to have a profound influence on its future.

Recollet Falls, looking north.

Could this be the "Fort" in the West Cross Channel?

In the early 1880s, the first settlers, many of them French-Canadians, came to the area north of the North Channel (Monetville, Noelville, Alban) where limited possibilities existed for agriculture. This influx of settlers was possible when the transcontinental Canadian Pacific Railway, coming from Ottawa, had reached North Bay on the northeast shore of Lake Nipissing in 1882. In 1886 the Grand Trunk Railway reached North Bay from Toronto. About this time tourists began to show up, coming to the Upper French River from North Bay across Lake Nipissing by sailboat or steamer, attracted to the superb fishing in a beautiful wilderness setting. Gradually, fishing and hunting resorts and lodges as well as summer camps and homes were beginning to appear in the Upper French River area. The hotels in French River Village not only catered to the logging business but also to visitors who came from big cities in Canada and the United States for the wild beauty of the northern wilderness and the excellent fishing in the French River. In 1886 a recommended canoe trip was to take the steamer to French River Village, paddle upriver for five days to North Bay, and then return south by rail.

Two rail lines were completed in 1908 connecting Sudbury with Toronto and crossing the French and Pickerel Rivers, one a kilometre west of Dry Pine Bay, and the other 11 kilometres west of Recollet Falls (see Map 5).

Because of the much-improved accessibility provided by these railroads, tourism began to take off, giving a boost to the construction of lodges, resorts, fishing and hunting clubs, and cottages. Postal services, telephone lines, and electricity were gradually introduced in the area.

In those days tourism was still mostly limited to the upper classes of society who had enough time and money to travel. But in 1954 the French River area was opened to less effluent visitors with the construction of Highway 69, which provided a direct connection between the South and Sudbury. In 1956–57 the Dokis Road, connecting Dokis Village with Highway 64 near Monetville, was built. The permanent population of the area increased as did the number of cottages, which today number more than eight hundred, spread out over the whole river but mainly concentrated in the vicinity of the highways. (See Maps 4 and 20.)

The French River became well known as a beautiful recreational area with an important and rich history. In 1986 it was designated Canada's first Canadian Heritage River and in 1989 much of the French River corridor received official park status as a Provincial Park. In 1992 a co-operative association, the Friends of French River Heritage Park, was established to assist in responsible management of the park.

That same year the Friends began to distribute a new map (made by the Ministry of Natural Resources). The 1:50,000-scale French River Provincial Park map, an improved and expanded edition of which was issued in 1995, made it possible to get a good overview of the delightful intricacies of the river system and to try to follow the routes taken by the fur traders so many years ago.

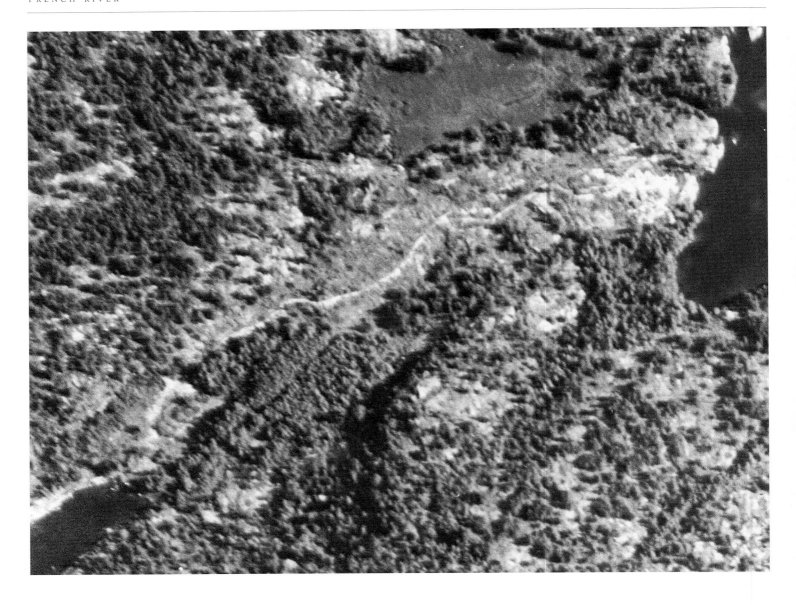

*Small detail of aerial
photograph made in 1946
showing the historic Chaudière
Portage.*

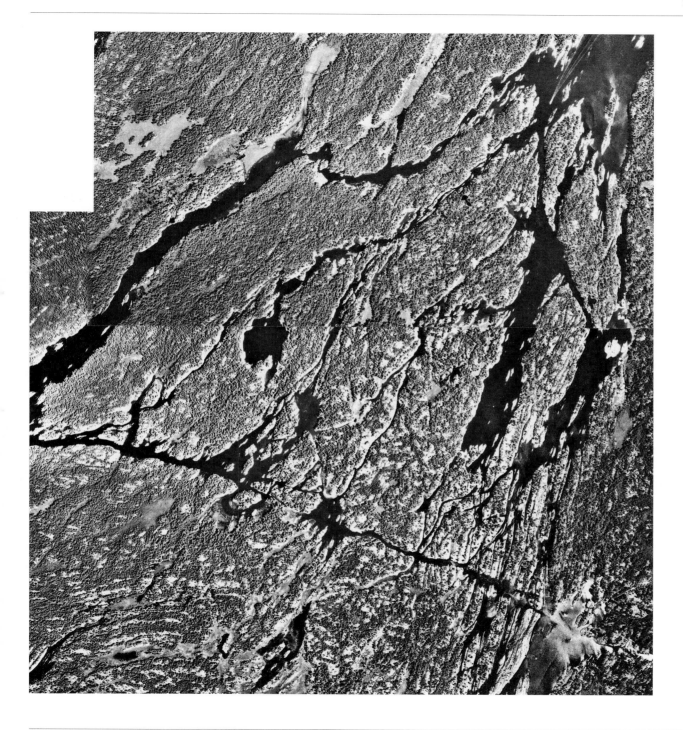

*Composite aerial
photograph of the
Western Outlets.*

Main Channel viewed downstream from the western end of Cross Island.

CHAPTER 6

HISTORIC CANOE ROUTES

O bviously, when speaking about the French River voyageur route, one is talking in general terms. The mouth of the river is complicated and offers too many options to restrict the travellers to one specific route. The paths the voyageurs chose would depend upon a number of factors including time of year, weather conditions, canoe type and loading, canoeing experience, brigade size, freight type, direction (upstream or downstream), and destination. But above all, water level was the overriding factor in deciding where to go and what to do on the river, and remains so to this day.

The voyageurs wanted to travel as quickly and efficiently as possible. They were in the business of transportation, of making money, and did not intend to waste precious time sightseeing, loafing around, or waiting for each other in traffic pile-ups.

Taking these factors into account and assuming that the water levels in those days followed roughly the same cycle they do now, a few broad conclusions can be made regarding the routes the fur-trade voyageurs might have used:

The route from Lake Nipissing down to Wanapitei Bay in the Delta would have been a straightforward following of the Main Channel after first crossing the Chaudière Portage into the river proper. At Wanapitei Bay the large fur-trade freight brigades would go south to the Main Outlet and descend or portage the Dalles Rapids. Groups of a few canoes and those not heavily loaded with trade goods (such as express canoes) would go to the Western Outlets and take the Old Voyageur Channel to Georgian Bay. The same procedures would be followed by canoes travelling upriver. However, if the water levels in the past were consistently higher than they are now, especially during spring high-water, greater numbers of the large freight canoes would have used the Old Voyageur Channel.

In several old trip journals, brief descriptions can be found of the routes selected by some past travellers, mostly dating from the British period after 1760. Place names are often inconsistent in these old documents. For instance, parts of the Main Channel have at various times been known as South Channel East, North Channel West, and Grand Recollet Channel. The Pickerel River was called South Channel East and Petite Recollet Channel. Several rapids, falls, and

Part of the first map showing the French River, made by Champlain in 1616 and published in updated form by Du Val in 1653 (7 = Lake Nipissing, 33 = French River).

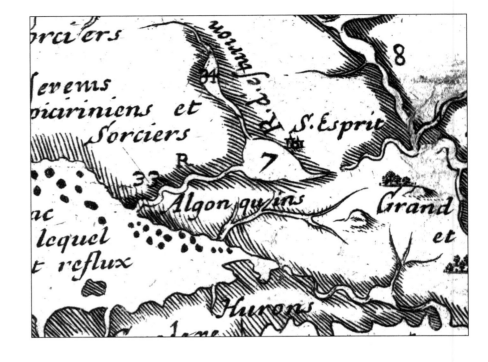

Section of Champlain's famous 1632 map (88 = French River).

Coronelli 1688 (detail).

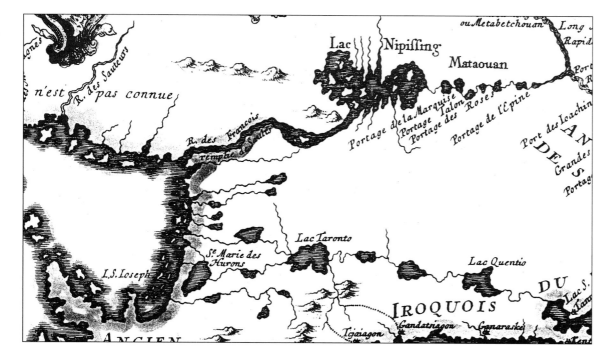

Bellin 1755 (detail).

Cary 1807 (detail).

Bouchette 1815 (detail). Note the various names of the rapids.

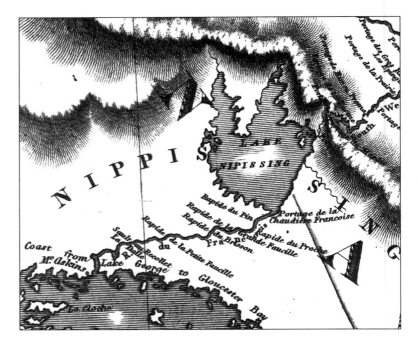

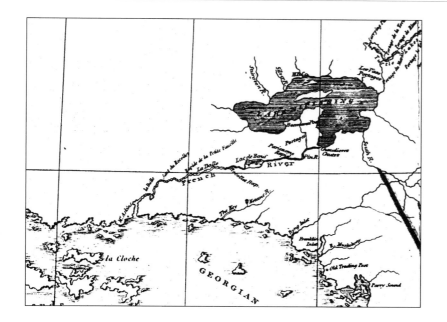

Part of a map made by Wyld in 1843 showing for the first time a rendition approaching the true shape of Lake Nipissing and the French River.

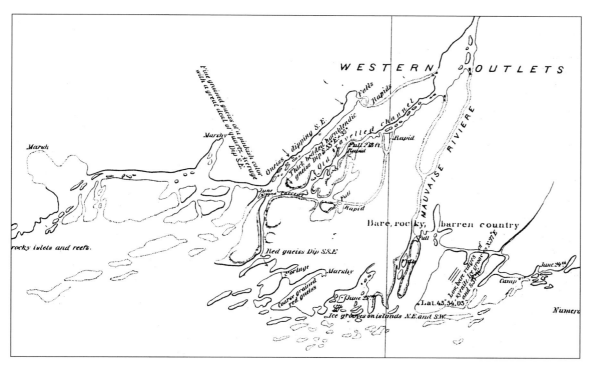

Detail of survey map made by Murray in 1847–1857 showing the Western Outlets, including the "Old Travelled Channel."

portages have also had different names (and even locations) over the years, which makes following the old reports and maps a difficult and time-consuming exercise.

To illustrate the gradual improvement in knowledge of the river's topography, a few reproductions of historic maps produced in the seventeenth to nineteenth centuries are provided, showing the French River and its surroundings. (See pages 94 to 97.)

The first map on which the French River can be easily recognized was made by Samuel de Champlain in 1616 and published in updated form in 1653 by Pierre Du Val. Champlain also produced a beautiful map in 1632 on which the French River is clearly indicated. Subsequent maps were becoming more accurate but names, locations, and shapes still tended to vary greatly.

In the second quarter of the nineteenth century, the first survey maps of the area were made by the Geological Survey of Canada. The first GSC topographical map of the whole French River was made by Murray between 1847 and 1857. Part of it (the Western Outlets) is reproduced on page 97, clearly showing the Old Travelled Channel, which was apparently the contemporary name for the Old Voyageur Channel. This was the first time this section of the voyageur route on the French River was indicated on a map.

In its 250 years as a crucial segment of the main fur-trade route, the French River was visited by uncounted thousands of canoes and paddlers. Surprisingly, very little physical evidence remains to show that these people indeed travelled the French River system. Several pre-contact Native archaeological sites have been discovered and these should yield interesting information once they are fully explored. But as far as the presence of non-Natives is concerned during the seventeenth to nineteenth centuries, no campsites, no notes, no graffiti, no marks, no footsteps, no garbage, no graves, practically no visible signs of any kind have ever been found along the shores of the river to attest to the passage of so many people. The only tangible proof that fur-trading canoeists were on the French River in past centuries are a number of artifacts found by divers below several rapids and falls since the early 1960s.

It is not surprising that fur-trade relics were found on the bottom of the river. Spills must have occurred once in a while when the coureurs de bois or the voyageurs would try to negotiate their heavily loaded canoes down the rapids instead of making a safe but time-consuming portage around them.

Credit for the first officially sanctioned and documented research in the waters of the French River goes to John Macfie, then Senior Conservation Officer in the Parry Sound office of the Ontario Department of Lands and Forests, who took the initiative to organize a small party to do some exploratory diving in the river in October 1961.

Macfie's two divers, Jim Sheppard and Don Hughson, were immediately successful in their first try. Below The Ladder, which in those days was also wrongly called Double Rapids, they found an impressive collection of durable trade goods including axes, kettles, musket balls and shot, glass beads, gunflints, fire steels, awls, ice chisels, knives, and one gun. In June 1962 more dives were attempted at various other places but nothing significant was found.

Frances Anne Hopkins: Running a Rapid on the Mattawa.

The finds from below The Ladder were handed over to the Royal Ontario Museum in Toronto for study, where the artifacts were identified as probably of French origin and dating from the late 1600s to about 1750.

From then on the research was taken over by Walter Kenyon of the ROM's Archaeology Department who, in 1963, 1966 (extensive searches), 1967, and 1971, systematically checked many locations from Wolseley Bay to the mouth of the river.

In most places nothing (or very little of importance) was found except in the Old Voyageur Channel, where several muskets were discovered, and below the Upper Parisien Rapids, where numerous artifacts (especially axes) dating from the British period were found. These and other occasional finds from various locations are all stored at the ROM.

Over the years, there have been quite a few unofficial finds made by amateur divers, who in many cases donated the artifacts to various museums but sometimes kept the relics for themselves. As the French River is a Provincial Park, removal, damaging, or defacing of any relic, artifact, or natural object is strictly forbidden.

Among the locations where underwater artifacts have been discovered are Third Rainy Rapids, The Ladder, Upper Parisien Rapids, Recollet Falls, Petite Faucille in the Old Voyageur Channel, and some unidentified sites in the Western Outlets. But the only really productive places on the entire French River turned out to be The Ladder and the Upper Parisien Rapids.

TRAVELLING WITH THE VOYAGEURS

The experience the voyageurs had in traversing these wild waters and lands was a very important

Frances Anne Hopkins: Shooting the Rapids.

factor in their decision-making process. The choice of which channel to take, of whether to run a rapid or to portage, of whether to unload partially or completely before lining or tracking the canoe, of whether to camp or to continue paddling, was made based on their extensive understanding of the French River at different times in the river's canoeing season (from May after ice break-up till the beginning of autumn early October) and at widely varying water levels and weather conditions.

They had to remain aware that their precious canoes were made of delicate birchbark, that their freight consisted of valuable goods such as packs of fur or trade goods and supplies, and that the people they sometimes transported to and from their western destination were usually unaccustomed to to the rigors of wilderness travel.

Probably very few of the passengers, or the voyageurs for that matter, could swim and life jackets had not yet been invented. The people must have had many frightening experiences during their long and arduous trips. If anything went wrong no outside help was available; the travellers were on their own in a vast and unforgiving wilderness that would offer no help to stranded people. Many of the passengers were dressed in tight, uncomfortable European clothing, complete with long-tailed coats, stiff collars, and fashionable high hats, making the ever-present bugs even more of a problem.

When trying to discover how canoeists in previous centuries went up and down the river, we will now accompany them in one of their canoes and apply the knowledge we have of canoeing, camping, and portaging techniques. The following imaginary trip with the voyageurs follows the five river sections introduced in Chapter 1.

Lake

In a typical year, the fur-trade brigades would have left Lachine after ice break-up in early May and arrived at the French River about three to four weeks later. For the voyageurs coming off the large expanse of Lake Nipissing, the Upper French River was a simple, 19-kilometre (12 miles)

*Upper Parisien Rapids at very
high water, looking south.*

flatwater paddle with little difficulty, although an occasional hard west wind could whip up the
water surface and create dangerously high waves. This had also been the case on wide-open Lake
Nipissing.

Dokis

The first obstacles the voyageurs encountered on their trip down the French River were the
unrunnable Chaudière Rapids, located at the top of the Main Channel of the river on the southeast side of Okikendawt Island, which forced the paddlers to make a portage. In their
centuries-long history on the river, the Native peoples had developed a simple, relatively short,
reasonably flat, and convenient trail leading from the west shore of Portage Bay (just east of the
Chaudière Rapids) to quiet Bruce Bay, which is part of the river proper. Once this portage was
pointed out to the Europeans, all of the traffic between Lake Nipissing and Georgian Bay began

to use this trail. It was the most effective way to move trade goods, fur, and people down and up the French River from May till October.

The length of the Chaudière Portage (as it is now called) is about 420 metres (1,380 feet) as measured on a 1946 aerial photograph where the trail is clearly visible on the light-colored rock (see page 90). This is fairly close to the 544 paces mentioned by Alexander Mackenzie in his book, *Voyages from Montreal*, about his 1789 and 1793 canoe trips to the west (see the excerpt on page 71).

This was also where, according to the oral tradition of the Dokis Band, Indian warriors occasionally tried to ambush the fur-trade brigades that passed through.

Tragically, the Chaudière Portage was all but destroyed in 1949 and 1950 by the construction of the dam-controlled Portage Channel. The trail is now to a large extent covered by rock debris, trees, and bush, and part of it has even been cut away by the channel itself. Only two sections at the beginning and end of it are still in reasonable shape, looking approximately like they did so many years ago.

There was another possibility for voyageurs wanting to get from the Upper French River to the river proper. They could stay north of Okikendawt Island and portage into the Little French River at the Little Chaudière Outlet or run the turbulent waters of the Freeflowing Channel (which has a portage on the east side) and then paddle around the island. But it is highly unlikely that the voyageurs would have ever taken that route because the Little French River adds quite a distance to the total trip length. Also the Five Finger Rapids, where the Little French empties into Wolseley Bay, are impossible to run. This would have forced the canoeists to traverse the Alligator Portage to the east, which would have added even more distance to the trip.

Once they had traversed the Chaudière Portage, the next potential problem the voyageurs encountered in the Main Channel was Cradle Rapids at Keso Point. If the water was very high it would create dangerous turbulence and crosscurrents below the Point. When going upstream in September, the rapids were probably easy to paddle or line up with a loaded boat because of low water. If necessary, the short Leonard Portage to the east could be used. But neither Keso Point nor Cradle Rapids are mentioned in the existing fur-trade literature, so the voyageurs likely did not encounter problems here.

From Keso Point down, the travellers then had an easy, 13-kilometre-long (8 miles) flatwater paddle to Wolseley Bay's Little Pine Rapids, the first of the Five Mile Rapids in the Main Channel running south of Eighteen Mile Island.

Island

Arriving at Commanda Island, the voyageurs had to decide whether to run Little Pine Rapids (which could be done at anything but very low water levels), to line the canoe down, or to portage for a short distance on the west shore. In 1968 a small rock island in the middle if the rapid was removed to increase the water flow at spring flood. Before that most of the water went down the large channel on the east side of the river but the smaller channel to the west of the island would also have been available for passage of the canoes. Going upriver it was probably easiest to line the fully loaded canoes up this smaller channel.

One kilometre (0.6 miles) further, the more impressive Big Pine Rapids forced the voyageurs to portage or line their canoes down (although skilled paddlers probably took the risk of running the rapid with an empty or partly loaded boat). In medium to high water this can be a fearsome rapid — doubly curved, with high waves, and potentially very dangerous. However, at very high water, despite its considerable standing waves, the water follows an almost straight path, which makes running it a possibility, especially in big canoes. There is a good portage trail on the west shore.

Although this Little Pine–Big Pine route is quite short, some of the voyageurs, given high enough water levels, may have taken the longer route around Commanda Island instead. They would have followed the Commanda Channel, running the three Rainy Rapids of which the last one might have caused problems as it is curved and has a ledge. There is no indication in the old literature that this route was taken by the voyageurs but it would have meant avoiding possible hard work on Little and Big Pine Rapids, something the men were of course always aiming at. Several artifacts found below the Third Rainy Rapids indicate that at least occasionally there had been travellers on the Commanda Channel. Going upriver, the Commanda Channel would probably not have offered much advantage over the other route.

After coming off Big Pine Rapids, the voyageurs ran the simple Double Rapids which would not cause any problems; these could easily be portaged, lined, poled, or waded if necessary, depending on the water level. They would then come to the remarkable Blue Chute, an exciting but essentially harmless run that the big boats could make downriver without much trouble — no hidden rocks, no curves, just a nice, straight channel marked by a smooth V, quite runnable by even the big canoes, which did not have much freeboard and could not be steered very well when fully loaded. They did have to stay out of the big standing waves in the middle of the chute or a disastrous swamping might have been the result.

*Lunch break on
the Little French River.*

Going up Blue Chute with a full cargo of precious fur meant some hard work for the voyageurs, who had to line their boats up. If need be, a difficult portage could be made over the small, hilly island west of Blue Chute, or they could try going up the narrow Gully if there was enough water.

Another option if the water was sufficiently high was to go down The Ladder instead, which diverts some of the water from the Main Channel just before Blue Chute. But this route, which consists of two separate, short rapids with some curved flow, was not really suitable for the big, heavily loaded boats. We know from successful underwater dives that The Ladder was run by fur-trade canoes, probably the smaller ones used by the coureur de bois.

The next whitewater section the travellers encountered was the Upper Parisien Rapids, which would present no problems if they were run with care. The whirlpools and big eddies in the pool below the rapids would not have had much effect on the big canoes. When the water level was very high and the river water spilled into a second channel to the south, much more diligence was required of the paddlers. If necessary, a portage could be made down a trail on the north shore. When going upriver a portage along this trail might have been necessary; lining up was another possibility.

Occasionally something must have gone wrong in the Upper Parisien Rapids because a rich assortment of artifacts has been discovered by divers in the deep pool below the rapids.

Lower Parisien Rapids, which follows less than 1 kilometre (0.6 miles) downriver, was easy. The south channel consists mostly of fast current and is unobstructed. Going upriver might have been difficult for the big fur-trade canoes because of the fast current, but lining along the north part of the rapids was a possibility.

Two kilometres (1.2 miles) further down, the voyageurs would come to the Crooked Rapids, an S-shaped channel that would be as smooth as glass in low water; however, when the water level was very high the turbulence and dangerous crosscurrents created by the mass of water going around the rocky corners at considerable speed would require extreme care. Negotiating tight curves in these big, heavily loaded canoes was not so simple. Going back upriver required portaging or lining when the water was high and the current strong, but at low water the voyageurs could easily paddle up the placid rapids.

The following 16 kilometres (10 miles) was a nice paddle down the Main Channel that would take the hard-working voyageurs no more than a couple of hours under favorable circumstances. A stiff west wind, often encountered here on these east–west stretches, made extra effort neces-

Frances Anne Hopkins: Canoe Manned by Voyageurs Passing a Waterfall.

sary. The travellers would pass several scenic landmarks that are well-known to visitors of the French River today: Cross Island, Haystack Islands, and Owl's Head Rock.

Arriving at Dalton's Point, which marks the entrance to Horseshoe Bay, the voyageurs either continued on the Main Channel (if they were going west to the Great Lakes) or turned south to the Pickerell River via Horseshoe Rapids and the hilly portage of Horseshoe Falls (if they went south to Huronia via the Pickerel River Outlet).

The fur-trade canoes of the voyageurs destined for Lake Superior or other points west would paddle around Lost Child Bend, arrive at Dry Pine Bay, and then turn west into the narrow Main Channel where The Swifts form a partial constriction. About 4 kilometres (2.5 miles) of paddling through a pretty section of the river called the French River Gorge, which is walled in by vertical cliffs, would bring them to the Recollet Falls.

It is unlikely that the fur traders would have followed the North Channel along the north side of Eighteen Mile Island. The various obstructions in this channel (Cedar Rapids and Chute, Ouellette Rapids, Meshaw Falls, and Stony Rapids) make it too difficult for big canoes. The paddling distance is also much greater on the North Channel than on the Main Channel.

Gorge

The scenic-but-notorious Recollet Falls could not be run by canoes at any water level and the voyageurs would have had to take out on the left side of the river, just a few metres above the falls which are about 2.1 metres (7 feet) high. At high water and strong current, this could be very dangerous indeed. If they were not extremely careful the current could easily sweep their heavily loaded boats down the nearby falls, leading to almost certain death for the unlucky travellers. There are various indications that Recollet Falls claimed quite a few casualties over the years. Several old artifacts have been found in these waters by divers, attesting to the danger of these falls.

The original portage trail was about 50 metres (165 feet) long and followed the same route as the present-day wooden boardwalk. The water coming off the falls flows against the vertical rockface on the south side of the river, which causes tricky crosscurrents and eddies that require great care when paddling across. The voyageurs in their heavy, deep-lying canoes would have had some anxious moments here.

Below Recollet Falls, the First and Second Rapids posed no real problems. The travellers only had to pay extra attention to avoid the sharp rocks just below the surface at low water levels.

Delta

From the Second Rapids down an easy flatwater paddle would bring the voyageurs to the Ox Bay–Wanapitei Bay area. Here a crucial decision had to be made regarding the route they should take, depending upon the level of the water. If the brigade guide thought that the water was high enough to carry the boats safely down the Old Voyageur Channel, they would continue west from Wanapitei Bay to the point where the Western Channel splits into the Western Outlets. But if the water level was considered to be too low, the voyageurs would turn south at Wanapitei Bay (or take the Canoe Channel at Ox Bay) into the Main Channel and follow it to the Main Outlet, where the Dalles Rapids form the last obstacle before the river waters flow into Georgian Bay.

At the Dalles the boats could be run or possibly lined down the relatively deep major channel on the south side without much of a problem. The water level was probably higher then, before the rock island in the middle of the channel was removed in 1962. If necessary (and this was likely to happen more often when going from the Bay back up to the river in September) the voyageurs could take the portage trail between Boiler Point Bay just above the rapids and Dalles Pool below them. Lining the canoes up the rapids was another possibility, especially attractive when the water was not too high. When going downriver, the standing waves that can exist in Little Dalles Rapids just below Dalles Pool when the river water level is high would not have posed any real problems for the big canoes.

It is unlikely that the voyageurs would have used the Eastern Outlet at Bass Lake, at the end of the Canoe Channel. It carries relatively little water, except in spring flood, and would not be suitable for the large canoes because its two exits are quite narrow and twisted.

If the Huron country to the south was the destination of the travellers and the water level was high enough, the Pickerel River (reached via Horseshoe Falls) was maybe the route to paddle. They could then follow the Pickerell River Outlet to Georgian Bay, saving a fair distance compared to descending the Main Outlet of the French River further west and then turning east and south.

However, this was such a difficult route to take at low water that most travellers to Huronia, and almost certainly the flotillas made up of many fur-carrying canoes from the Hurons on their way to the St. Lawrence, would have taken the Main Outlet, in spite of the somewhat longer travel distance.

If the voyageurs decided at Wanapitei Bay that the river water level was high enough to run one of the outlet channels of the Western Outlets, they would have continued west via the Western Channel. This meant a comfortable 14-kilometre (9 miles) paddle to The Junction, where the Western Channel transforms into the delta of the Western Outlets, which consists of three main outlet channels: the Bad River Channel, the Old Voyageur Channel, and the Voyageur Channel.

If the Bad River Channel was selected, the easiest run down was through the Boat Channel and then the East Branch; the First and Second Swifts would not have posed any problems for the big canoes. Of the several secondary outlets coming out of the upper Bad River Channel and dropping into the High Cross Channel three can be used by big canoes: Herring Chute, Lily Chutes, and Crooked Rapids. The last one is the simplest if approached very carefully and at the right water level (low but not too low). It is the only one of the three where no portaging or lining is required to get the canoes down to the High Cross Channel. From there Georgian Bay can be reached via the Big or Little Jameson Rapids or the Devil's Door, which is a very dangerous drop except at low water level.

Both Herring Chute and Lily Chutes have seen large modern fibreglass canoes lined down with great care but this does not mean that birchbark canoes would have been subjected to the same treatment by the voyageurs. Paddling up The Jump at the bottom of Crooked Rapids, the rapids themselves, and then the rest of the upper Bad River Channel is not easy in big canoes, but it can be done at low water level if the canoes are not too heavily loaded. The Back Channel, splitting off Crooked Rapids, is not suitable for big canoes because of its curved north entry. Because of all these difficulties, the Bad River Channel and its outlets were probably not used by the big fur-trade canoes, although smaller canoes must have been there as some old artifacts have been discovered in this area.

West of the Bad River Channel is the Old Voyageur Channel which, according to several historic sources, was the principal route of the voyageurs. On Murray's 1847–1857 survey map it is marked as the "Old Travelled Channel" (see page 97). However, closer study of this route from a canoeing point of view reveals some serious difficulties that would have been encountered by travellers in big canoes, limiting the use of this route to periods of sufficiently high water levels. This would especially have been the case with large brigades going upriver.

There are four places in the Old Voyageur Channel that, depending upon the water level, are potential trouble spots for big canoes. The first is the East Channel of the Rock Circus, a narrow, almost-straight passage between sloping rock walls and connected to the western part of the Rock Circus by three openings through which water can flow. (In some studies this channel is called La Dalle, but the true location of that section appears to be further down the Old Voyageur Channel.)

The East Channel is an interesting passage with obvious possibilities for canoe travel but unfortunately several rocks sticking up from the channel floor obstruct canoe traffic at medium-to-low water. Even at relatively high water the big voyageur boats, lying deep because of their heavy loads, would not have been able to negotiate this channel without running serious risks. This channel would have been used by fur traders only at quite high water levels. Upriver travel would have been difficult because of the strong current as well as the steep walls of the narrow East Channel, which would have made lining up troublesome.

The second obstacle in the Old Voyageur Channel is the Petite Faucille (Little Sickle), an unrunnable drop with an average height of less than a metre (3 feet), where the canoes had to be unloaded and carried over the rocky peninsula to the south for about 20 metres (66 feet). The existence of the Petite Faucille is mentioned a few times in the notes of several of the old travellers. The artifacts found in the late 1960s on the river bottom below the drop are another indication that this route was used by the fur traders. In his 1845 painting, *French River Rapids*, Paul Kane gives a curious artist's impression of what presumably is the Petite Faucille.

The third serious obstacle in the Old Voyageur Channel, the Palmer Rocks, can cause severe problems for passing travellers

Paul Kane: French River Rapids.

Frances Anne Hopkins:
Tracking the Rapids (*detail*).

if the water level is not high enough. They consist of a rock ridge made up of several parts crossing the channel at an angle, and make it practically impossible for big boats to pass in low-to-medium water levels. Portaging this section is extremely difficult because of the inhospitable terrain.

Finally, a few hundred metres below the Palmer Rocks, the voyageurs encountered a scenic and comfortably straight channel about 100 metres (330 feet) long that could be run at any water level by canoes of all sizes. Going upriver at high water levels the big boats could be lined up against the strong current by walking on top of the elevated west bank. This is probably the famous La Dalle mentioned in several of the old trip journals, although it is not impossible that in the fur-trade days the whole Old Voyageur Channel was sometimes called La Dalle and not just any small section of it.

Below La Dalle, the waters flow into the West Cross Channel and the travellers would have to decide whether to go west on this channel or to take the Fort Channel directly to Georgian Bay.

We can conclude that the Old Voyageur Channel was probably only used by the voyageurs at quite high water levels and not by the big brigades of fur trade canoes. Smaller fur-trade canoes and specialized big canoes carrying only passengers, mail, and other important cargo would also have used this channel. These express or light canoes had less weight to carry and therefore enjoyed more freeboard to run rapids and shallow parts. They were also easier to handle in the narrow channels and to portage.

The westernmost outlet of the French River is called Voyageur Channel, which seems to suggest that the voyageurs travelled this channel on a regular basis. But this is very unlikely from a canoeing point of view. There are too many obstructions, especially at the upstream end of the channel where several rock formations almost completely block access for big canoes. Guiding canoes through here would have been very difficult indeed if there was not sufficient water. There are no reports in the old journals indicating use of this channel by the fur traders.

Once the voyageurs had reached Georgian Bay through whatever river outlet they had selected, their troubles were not over. The north and east shores of Georgian Bay are famous for the myriad rocks in the water, many of them just below the surface, waiting to strand unsuspecting paddlers and boaters (and possibly destroying their craft in the process). The weather in these parts can also play nasty tricks, changing to storms and high winds on very short notice and creating huge waves. The danger of accidents was always present and the voyageurs had to be extremely careful — and above all needed experienced guides — when negotiating these hazardous waters.

The voyageurs would have encountered a serious complication when returning from the West at the end of September or early October. They would immediately have to decide on the correct channel to take the canoes back upriver without knowing the actual water level in the river. The choice would have to depend upon their intimate knowledge and understanding of the weather and the topography of the country.

Using the Old Voyageur Channel had several advantages over the Main Outlet via the Dalles Rapids. For one thing, they would not have to travel as far along the treacherous section of the Georgian Bay north shore. They would also have easy access to the far western end of the West Cross Channel where the reputed Prairie des Français would have offered shelter in case of inclement weather. Of course, they also ran the risk of being ambushed at the Fort.

Very little information exists about locations along the French River where the fur traders might have camped. There must have been several campsites — quite large ones to accommodate the often considerable number of canoes — because of the time it would have taken to travel the river. Under the right circumstances the voyageurs paddling express canoes could apparently go downriver in one day, as mentioned in several of the old journals. But going upriver, especially at high water, the trip would have taken several days. The regular big freight canoes would surely have needed a few days to travel the river with all of the cargo that had to be portaged.

When we retrace the routes of the voyageurs, it is impossible to do so without feeling immense respect for the achievements of these hardy people with their unsophisticated equipment, clothing, food, and maps.

La Dalle in the Old Voyageur Channel at low water, Western Outlets, looking northeast.

CHAPTER 7

SUGGESTED CANOE TRIPS

PREPARATIONS

The French River system has many attractive features that make it appealing for canoe and kayak trippers today. A large variety of trips of different duration and degree of difficulty is possible, from easy flatwater during the whole canoeing season to challenging whitewater at spring break-up. There are several convenient road access points including public docks and well-equipped commercial marinas and lodges. Many closed-loop trips can be made, avoiding the need for car shuttles. Lodge-to-lodge canoe trips can also be organized and there are numerous opportunities for exploring places rarely visited by humans. The river system has a diverse landscape, the fishing is excellent, and it has a unique and fascinating history going back long before the explorers, missionaries, and fur traders travelled the river.

The magical days when the French River system was a true wilderness where few people wandered are long past. Now, especially in the more popular locations such as Wolseley Bay, Eighteen Mile Bay, Dry Pine Bay, Hartley Bay, and surrounding areas, there will be other canoeists, boaters, cottagers, and fishers doing their thing. But there are still plenty of remote, practically untouched places full of wildness and natural beauty to be found by those who know where to look.

The pamphlet "French River Visitors Code of Ethics," researched, produced, and published by the Friends of French River Heritage Park and available free of charge at most access points and other locations in the area, offers many tips that will help improve the quality of your visit and keep the river a safe, clean, beautiful place. Remember that the French River is a Heritage River and that much of it is also Provincial Park, so don't disturb or remove historical artifacts and natural objects such as wildflowers. Although most of the French River area consists of public and Crown lands, there are also two Native First Nations and other private properties, homes, cottages, resorts, lodges, and marinas that need to be respected.

There are dangers involved when visiting the lands and waters of the French River system. Bears and rattlesnakes are really the least of your problems if you follow a few basic common-sense rules. The greatest dangers in canoe tripping in remote places lie in twisting an ankle, getting sunstroke, tangling with poison ivy, suffering from food poisoning, even getting a grain of sand in your eye — anything that requires immediate medical attention.

The water quality of the river is satisfactory for swimming; however, as far as drinking the water is concerned, it should be treated by boiling or by adding purification chemicals.

The French River system is complex. As such the possible combinations of canoe routes are almost infinite. A number of representative trips are therefore suggested along with some basic information to help you organize and experience the kind of adventure you're looking for. These trip outlines are followed by some essential details on most of the rapids, falls, and portages you will encounter.

Much of the magic of canoe tripping lies in discovering for yourself what this demanding but highly satisfying activity is all about. So, beyond these trip suggestions you're on your own. Use your imagination and collect as much information as possible to prepare yourself and your partners as best you can. Select a likely route from those mentioned below and make your own variations if necessary. Different trips can be combined into one and sections of suggested trips can be done on their own. Use maps and aerial photographs to discover interesting details of your selected route. (See under Aerial Photographs and Maps in the Main Sources section.)

The French River Provincial Park map is excellent and also gives the location of officially sanctioned campsites, but be aware that, like all maps, it is not perfect. Never trust any map implicitly; they are only meant to help you find your way in unknown country and should not be used as infallible guides. Always use your common sense and base your decisions on what you see with your own eyes. Nothing beats experience.

Use the material presented earlier in this book about the topography and history of the river. The area will come alive and make your adventure more meaningful.

It's impossible to give advice on the *best* time for canoe tripping; that is too personal a choice. Some people prefer the wild waters of May (and don't mind the black-flies and mosquitoes that may be out for their blood), others enjoy the quiet days of late September and early October with their exhilarating fall colors and crispy nights. The summer months see the most people on the water but there are great days to be spent on the French River any time of the open-water season, from late April to early December, when freeze-up begins.

Two different kinds of road access points are available from which you can start your trip: public (free-of-charge docks without supervised parking) and commercial (marinas and lodges that charge a small fee for launching your canoe and keeping your car in a guarded lot). (Most of the existing access points are marked on Map 20 together with their telephone numbers if available.) Before you start your trip, contact the access point of your choice for important information about water levels, the availability of a grocery store, car shuttle, road taxi (to get you to your starting point by car), water taxi (to get you to a remote part of the system by motor boat), on-site camping, canoe rental and outfitting opportunities. (See Map 20 for several canoe-rental places on Highway 69.)

Let the people managing your access point know what your plans and schedule are so that, in case you are late in returning (for whatever reason), they can alert the authorities to try to locate you. Some access points may even have cellular phones for use in emergencies.

Trips

The following route outlines are presented by approximate trip duration and then roughly going downriver from east to west. (See Map 20 for access points [AP].) Some trips follow that include areas just outside of the French River area.

The suggested trips will take anywhere from one day to more than two weeks. But these durations are rough estimates, you may decide how slow or fast you want to travel. To enjoy this river and the surrounding country to the fullest it is best to do a long-duration, short-distance trip. Incorporate as many layover days as you can; this will give you the opportunity to take it easy and explore to your heart's content.

Delightful side trips can be made by portaging into lakes, marshes, and creeks away from the existing routes. Be adventurous, explore areas on the other side of the river banks, seldom visited by people. An easy paddling tempo of about 3 to 4 kilometres per hour (2–2.5 miles per hour) during windless days on flatwater is comfortable for most recreational trippers. A good day could see you travel from 15 to 20 kilometres (10–13 miles) but be aware that rapids and portages can require quite a lot of extra time. Also, reserve some time to look for campsites at the end of the day if you are unfamiliar with the area, because these are generally not marked on the river banks.

An important word of advice: the quality of the trip and the amount of danger you're submitting yourself and your partners to depend to a considerable extent upon the water level of the river. This is especially the case during May and June when the level can vary tremendously in a short period of time. However, unexpected fluctuations can and will occur throughout the season. After heavy rain storms the level can easily go up 20 centimetres (8 inches) or more in several hours, depending upon the location. So always keep an eye open for water-level changes.

Also, never assume that the water level will remain constant overnight when you camp on the shore. Pull your canoe up well above the high-water mark.

ONE DAY

Numerous short trips can be made from any access point in several directions and back to the access point, for instance:

Portage Channel AP 1a and 1b. East and south to Portage Channel and Big Chaudière Dam, explore area. About 10 kilometres (6 miles). No rapids.

Hunt Island AP 1c. Up Upper French River between islands on north side and then around Hunt Island. About 14 kilometres (9 miles). No rapids.

Freeflowing Channel AP 1d. West to Freeflowing Channel, explore area. About 16 kilometres (10 miles). No rapids.

Restoule Bay AP 2. Explore Restoule Bay and Main Channel between Portage Channel and Wolseley Bay. No rapids.

Wolseley Bay area AP 3. Explore Five Finger Rapids, Commanda Channel, Little Pine Rapids, or Cedar Rapids.

Dry Pine Bay area AP 4, 5, or 6. Visit Recollet Falls, Stony Rapids, Lost Child Bend or Little French Rapids. (There is an interesting hike to the Recollet Falls via a strenuous 1.5-kilometre (1 mile) trail starting at the parking lot where Highway 69 crosses the French River.)

Pickerel River AP 8. Visit Little French Rapids and Horseshoe Falls. About 13 kilometres (8 miles). No rapids.

Pickerel River AP 9. Downriver and then around McDougal Island. About 18 kilometres (11 miles). No rapids.

Fraser Bay AP 10. Hartley Bay, north into Allen Lake, east into Fraser Bay. About 16 kilometres (10 miles). No rapids.

Ox Bay AP 10. Hartley Bay, south into Wanapitei Bay, east into Ox Bay. About 16 kilometres (10 miles). No rapids.

TWO TO THREE DAYS

Upper French River AP 1. This flatwater area is filled with islands and bays that can be explored in many different ways and directions. For instance, paddle upriver between islands on north side

*Stamp Channel in the
Voyageur Channel at low
water, Western Outlets,
looking north.*

to Burnt Island and back. About 40 kilometres (25 miles).

Wolseley Bay area AP 3. Visit Cedar Rapids, Little Pine Rapids, Commanda Channel, Five Finger Rapids, and islands in Wolseley Bay.

Commanda Island loop AP 3. Commanda Channel, explore lower section of Nemesagamesing River, Main Channel, up Big and Little Pine Rapids. About 20 kilometres (12 miles) with five or more rapids.

Blue Chute and back AP 3. Main Channel or Commanda Channel, Blue Chute, visit Upper Parisien Rapids and return, up The Ladder, Main Channel, up Big and Little Pine Rapids or Commanda Channel. About 20 kilometres (12 miles) with nine or more rapids.

Crooked Rapids and back AP 3. Wolseley Bay, Main Channel or Commanda Channel, Five Mile Rapids to Crooked Rapids, visit Hammerhead Bay, return up Five Mile Rapids, The Ladder, up Big and Little Pine Rapids or Commanda Channel. About 30 kilometres (19 miles) with twelve or more rapids.

North Channel to Dry Pine Bay AP 3. Down North Channel, Eighteen Mile Bay, Stony Rapids, Dry Pine Bay. About 45 kilometres (28 miles) with six rapids. Car shuttle needed. Can also be done in reverse direction.

Main Channel to Dry Pine Bay AP 3. Five Mile Rapids and Main Channel, Lost Child Bend or Canoe Channel, Dry Pine Bay. About 40 kilometres (25 miles) with seven rapids. Car shuttle needed. Can also be done in reverse direction.

Cantin Island loop AP 4, 8, or 9. For instance: AP 8. Up Pickerel River, portage Horseshoe Falls and Rapids, Horseshoe Bay, west on Main Channel, Deer Bay, portage Little French Rapids, Pickerel River. About 20 kilometres (12 miles) with three rapids.

Across Eighteen Mile Island AP 4, 5, 6, or 7. For instance: AP 6. Dry Pine Bay, portage Stony Rapids, Eighteen Mile Bay, North Channel, turn south at Ash Bay, cross island via Pike Lake and Island Lake using unmarked and rarely used portages, west on Main Channel, Dry Pine Bay. About 50 kilometres (31 miles) with several portages. Can also be done in reverse direction.

Fourteen Mile Island loop AP 4, 5, 8, or 9. For instance: AP 5. Down Main Channel, Ox Bay, Pickerel River, portage Little French Rapids or Horseshoe Falls and Rapids, Main Channel. About 50 kilometres (31 miles) with two or three rapids.

North Delta AP 10. Flatwater exploration of many bays and channels, including Allen Lake, Fraser Bay, falls of Wanapitei River, lower Wanapitei River, Thompson Bay, Western Channel, Main Channel and Outlet, Canoe Channel, Eastern Outlet, Ox Bay, lower Pickerel River. No rapids.

Hartley Bay to Pickerel River AP 10. Wanapitei Bay, up Pickerel River to AP 8 or 9. About 30 kilometres (19 miles). No rapids. Car shuttle needed. Can also be done in reverse direction.

Hartley Bay to Key River AP 10. Wanapitei Bay, Pickerel River, Pickerel River Outlet, Georgian Bay islands, up Key River to AP 11. About 40 kilometres (25 miles) with three rapids. Car shuttle needed. Can also be done in reverse direction.

FIVE TO SEVEN DAYS

Upper French River AP 1. Extended flatwater exploration of area filled with islands and bays. For instance, visit Five Mile Bay, Bobs Bay, Twilight Bay, Hunters Bay, and Marsh Bay on north side, and Hardy Bay, Satchels Bay, and Frank's Bay on south side.

Okikendawt loop AP 1. West to Little French River, Freeflowing Channel or Little Chaudière Dam or Hall Chute, Little French River, explore Five Finger Rapids, long Five Fingers Portage or short Alligator Portage, Wolseley Bay, up Main Channel, Keso Point or Leonard Portage, Bruce Bay, explore Chaudière Rapids area, modern portage to Upper French. About 45 kilometres (28 miles) with three rapids. Can also be done in reverse direction and when starting from AP 2 or 3.

Dokis to Hartley Bay AP 1. Modern portage around Portage Channel, Main Channel, Five Mile Rapids, Main Channel, Dry Pine Bay, Main Channel, Wanapitei Bay, Hartley Bay, AP 10. About 75 kilometres (47 miles) with nine rapids. Car shuttle needed. Can also be done in reverse direction.

Dokis to Pickerel River AP 1. As above to Dalton's Point in Main Channel, Horseshoe Bay, Horseshoe Rapids and Falls, west on Pickerel River to AP 8 or 9. About 55 kilometres (34 miles) with ten rapids. Car shuttle needed. Can also be done in reverse direction.

Wolseley Bay – Delta – Key River AP 3. Main Channel, Wanapitei Bay, Main Outlet, Dalles Rapids, Georgian Bay islands, east to Key River, AP 11. About 100 kilometres (62 miles) with nine rapids. Car shuttle needed. Can also be done in reverse direction.

Eighteen Mile Island loop Any access point along route (or from AP 3). For instance: AP 6. Up Stony Rapids, Eighteen Mile Bay, up North Channel, Wolseley Bay, Commanda Channel or Main Channel, Five Mile Rapids, Main Channel, Dry Pine Bay. About 70 kilometres (44 miles) with thirteen rapids. Can also be done in reverse direction, but Five Mile Rapids can be difficult going upriver at high water level.

Dry Pine Bay - Delta - Key River AP 5 or 6. Main Channel, Wanapitei Bay, Main Outlet and Dalles Rapids (or any outlet in Western Outlets via Western Channel), Georgian Bay islands, east to Key River, AP 11. About 65 kilometres (41 miles) with two rapids. Car shuttle needed. Can also be done in reverse direction.

Pickerel River to Key River AP 8 or 9. Pickerel River, Pickerel River Outlet, Georgian Bay islands, Key River, AP 11. About 50 kilometres (31 miles) with four rapids. Car shuttle needed. Can also be done in reverse direction. (It is possible to continue and get back on the Pickerel River via Grundy Lake Provincial Park and the Pakeshag River if there is enough water.)

South Delta AP 10. Wanapitei Bay, The Junction at Western Outlets (consider hiring a water taxi), Old Voyageur Channel or any other outlet, West Cross Channel west to Indian Bay, south to Georgian Bay islands, east along coast, Bustard Islands, Dead Island, up Pickerel River Outlet, Ox Bay, Wanapitei Bay, Hartley Bay. About 75 kilometres (47 miles) with seven rapids. Caution: Georgian Bay is unpredictable and can be very dangerous; take a compass and good maps and be aware of quickly changing weather.

South Delta AP 8 or 9. Down Pickerel River (consider hiring a water taxi), Pickerel River Outlet, west to Georgian Bay islands, Bustard Islands, up Eastern Outlet, Dalles Rapids, down Main Outlet, west on East Cross Channel, up any of the Western Outlets, Western Channel, Ox Bay, Pickerel River. About 95 kilometres (59 miles) with ten rapids.

South Delta AP 4, 5, 8, 9, 10, or 11. Explore rarely visited area between Pickerel River Outlet and Main Outlet. Many unnamed inlets, islands, bays, and marshes with narrow, interconnecting channels and creeks. Ideal for adventurous trippers who want to experience truly wild country.

Western Outlets AP 10. Western Channel, in Western Outlets make camp and explore area, visit numerous small creeks and channels where few people ever set foot, see for yourself the places where the voyageurs travelled, return to access point via Western Channel, Main Outlet, or Eastern Outlet.

TEN TO FOURTEEN DAYS

Dokis – Georgian Bay – Dry Pine Bay AP 1 or 2. Main Channel (or Little French River), Wolseley Bay, Five Mile Rapids, Main Channel, Wanapitei Bay, Western Channel, Old Voyageur Channel or other outlet, turn east Georgian Bay islands, up Main Outlet, Canoe Channel, Ox Bay, Pickerel River, portage Horseshoe Falls, Horseshoe Bay, Dry Pine Bay. About 150 kilometres (95 miles) with fourteen rapids. Car shuttle needed. Can also be done in reverse.

MORE THAN FOURTEEN DAYS

North Bay to Georgian Bay and back Access point at Champlain Park on mouth of LaVase River, across Lake Nipissing or along south coast, Upper French River, portage to Bruce Bay, Main Channel, Wolseley Bay, North Channel, Dry Pine Bay, Main Channel, Wanapitei Bay, Western Channel, Old Voyageur Channel, west on West Cross Channel, Georgian Bay islands, turn east, up Main Outlet, Dalles Rapids, down Eastern Outlet, Georgian Bay islands, turn east, up Pickerell River Outlet, east on Pickerel River, Horseshoe Falls, Horseshoe Bay, Main Channel, Five Mile Rapids, Wolseley Bay, Five Finger Rapids, Little French River, Little Chaudière Dam, Upper French River, Lake Nipissing back to North Bay. About 300 kilometres (190 miles) with twenty-one rapids. This is the ultimate French River trip.

TRIPS INCLUDING AREAS OUTSIDE OF FRENCH RIVER SYSTEM

Restoule loop AP 1 or 2. Northeast on Upper French River to Frank's Bay, up Shoal Creek, Bass Lake, Restoule Provincial Park, down Restoule River. Can also be accessed from Restoule Provincial Park.

Nemesagamesing loop AP 2 or 3. Commanda Channel, up Nemesagamesing River, Nemesagamesing Lake, down Restoule River.

Mercer loop Public access point at west end of Mercer Lake near Highway 64, Hall River, portage to Little French River, Wolseley Bay, take out at Wolseley Bay Village and do car shuttle, or continue up Wolseley River, Bear Lake, Deer Bay, West Bay, Lake Nipissing, Upper French River, up Hall River, Mercer Lake.

Pickerel River AP 4, 5, or 6. Up Main Channel to narrow bay 2 kilometres (1.2 miles) east of Cross Island, turn southwest into bay, T Bay, portage to Pickerel River, turn west to complete loop to access point, or turn east to explore upper Pickerel River and Wolf River.

Key River to Killarney AP 11. West on Key River, explore Georgian Bay islands and north coast, Killarney village. Good trip for sea kayaks.

Murdoch loop AP 5 or 6. Up Murdoch River to Round Lake, west crossing Highway 69, Kakakiwaganda Lake, south to Commodore Lake, Bayswater Lake, La Casse Lake, Wanapitei Bay, up Main Channel, Dry Pine Bay.

Wanapitei River Access at Highway 637 bridge, down Wanapitei River, Wanapitei Bay or Thompson Bay, east to various access points, or west to Killarney via Western Outlets.

RAPIDS, FALLS, PORTAGES

Many French River rapids can be run under the right circumstances, given enough experience and the correct equipment. But always scout the whitewater sections yourself because the situation may have changed since the last time you were there.

All rapids and falls in the French River area can be bypassed by portages varying from short and easy to long and difficult. So don't worry that you'll get stuck somewhere; there's always a way to get out.

Dokis

MAIN CHANNEL Both **Chaudière Rapids** are unrunnable and blocked by dams; take modern portage starting at south end of Portage Bay, 600 metres (660 yards) to Bruce Bay. **Cradle Rapids** are no problem at low water level, at high water level take short **Leonard Portage** across peninsula east of Keso Point.

LITTLE FRENCH RIVER Run **Freeflowing Channel** (experienced paddlers) or portage 70 metres (77 yards) on east shore. **Little Chaudière Dam** portage 50 metres (55 yards) across island on west side. **Hall Chute** is runnable at right water level, there is a simple lift-over below. **Five Finger Rapids** are unrunnable, take difficult 300-metre (330 yards) portage on west shore or easy **Alligator Portage** 60 metres (66 yards) across peninsula to east.

Island

COMMANDA CHANNEL Run **First Rainy Rapids** or portage 30 metres (33 yards) on north shore. **Flat Rainy Rapids** is a rock garden, wade or run. **Third Rainy Rapids** is curved with ledge, runnable by experienced paddlers at high water level, portage 40 metres (44 yards) on north shore.

MAIN CHANNEL Run, wade, or line **Little Pine Rapids** or portage 40 metres (44 yards) on west shore; explore high-water channel on east shore. Run **Big Pine Rapids** or portage 80 metres (88 yards) on west shore. Run, wade, or line **Double Rapids** or portage 40 metres (44 yards) on west shore. **The Ladder** is only runnable at high water level, take two portages on west shore or explore portage on east shore. **Blue Chute** can be run by experienced paddlers at all water levels, or take difficult 120-metre (132 yards) portage across island on north side. Run first part of **The Gully** if water level high enough, followed by short portage on south side across island; this channel is dry at low water level. Run **Upper Parisien Rapids** with care or portage 80 metres (88 yards) on north shore, dangerous rapids at high water level, beware of whirlpools and eddies in pool below. **Lower Parisien Rapids** has fast current in main channel on south side, runnable rapids on north side when water level high enough. Curved flow of **Crooked Rapids** is difficult at high water level, take portage across peninsula on north shore.

HORSESHOE BAY Run **Horseshoe Rapids** if water level is high enough, at low water level portage on west shore or across rock debris in middle. Do not run **Horseshoe Falls** but take rocky 60-metre (66 yards) portage on west shore.

DEER BAY Do not run **Little French Rapids** but take 220-metre (242 yards) portage on south shore or explore rough portage on north shore.

NORTH CHANNEL Run **First Cedar Rapids** or line on north side. Run **Second Cedar Rapids** or line or portage on north side. Run **Third Cedar Rapids** or line or portage in middle. Run **Cedar Chute** or line or portage on north side. **Ouellette Rapids** has big standing waves at high water level, take short portage on north shore. Portage **Meshaw Falls** on south shore but ask permission first. **Stony Rapids** is runnable but has big standing waves at high water level, take 70-metre (77 yards) portage on south shore or explore seldom-used portage on north shore.

Gorge

MAIN CHANNEL Run **The Swifts** on north side, watch out for motorboats. **Recollet Falls** is dangerous drop, do not run, portage 50 metres (55 yards) on boardwalk on south shore, difficult take-out especially at high water level (maybe try rather awkward take-out about 40 metres (44 yards) upstream on south shore), watch out for eddies and cross-currents in turbulent flow below falls. **First Rapids** and **Second Rapids** watch for rocks at low water level.

Delta

PICKEREL RIVER OUTLET **East Channel Rapids** (in main canoeing channel) have two short portages on west shore at low water level but at high water level one hilly 300-metre (330 yards) portage on west shore, followed by 60-metre (66 yards) portage bypassing several small pools. **West Channel Rapids** have two short and rarely used portages on south shore at end of channel.

EASTERN OUTLET Approaches to **Bass Creek Falls** and **Bass Creek West Exit** are narrow, twisted, and hard to access especially at low water level, but interesting to explore; take 250-metre (275 yards) boardwalk on the east shore.

MAIN OUTLET Run **Dalles Rapids** (experienced paddlers) or line on south side, wade or carry on north side (at low water level), or portage 180 metres (198 yards) on south shore. **Little Dalles Rapids** standing waves at high water level only.

WESTERN OUTLETS **First Swift** fast current at high water level, portage **Otter Rapids** in Otter Channel if paddling upriver. **Second Swift** fast current at high water level, take short portage on east shore if going upriver. Run **Herring Chute** with care or line or lift over on east shore. **Lily Chutes** dangerous, do not run, line with great care on west shore. **Farley Portage** can be tried if water level high enough to get close to it. Run **Crooked Rapids** with caution because it is regularly used in both directions by many motorboats. **The Jump** can be a high hydraulic step at high water level. **Back Channel** difficult north entry from Crooked Rapids, run with great care because of possible motorboats. **Hassie Portage** is safe and simple way to get to and from High Cross Channel at all water levels. Run or line **Lovers Rapids**. **Lovers Falls** dangerous to run, lining difficult because of high sidewalls. **Devil's Door** can be a high hydraulic step, only run at very low

Taking it easy. Several canoes tied together sailing up the Canoe Channel in the Delta.

water level, in emergency take short but difficult **Devil's Door Portage** to north. Run or line **Little Jameson Rapids** or take rough portage to east. Run or line **Big Jameson Rapids** (can be dangerous at high water level). Run or line **Harris Rapids**. **Herb's Falls** are narrow, do lift-over on east side. **Cross Channel Rapids** has ledge; run, wade, or line. **Rock Circus** and **East Channel** can be run at adequate water level only. **Boston Falls** narrow and unrunnable, difficult portage on west shore. **Petite Faucille** 20-metre (22 yards) portage across peninsula on south side, run with care at high water level. Run **Palmer Rocks** at adequate water level only. Run **La Dalle** at any water level, when going upriver at high water level line on west shore. **Mushroom Channel** unrunnable. **Marten Cut** lift-over across rock ridge. Run **Stamp Channel** at adequate water level, can be dry at low water level. Run **Washer Woman** at low water level, big hydraulic step possible at high water level.

Always keep in mind that the Georgian Bay water level can have a significant influence on the quality and character of several of the exits.

If you hear or see any unfamiliar whitewater coming up, remember the first golden rule of canoe tripping: When in doubt, get out, and scout!

MAIN SOURCES

Acres International Ltd. *Lake Nipissing / French River Operational Guidelines*. Draft Report to Public Works and Government Services Canada. Toronto: February 1995.

Adney, Edwin Tappan, and Howard I. Chapelle. *The Bark Canoes and Skin Boats of North America*. Washington D.C.: Smithsonian Institution Press, 1983.

Aerial photographs. Ontario Ministry of Natural Resources, Toronto.

Barlow, A.E. *Second Edition of a Report on the Geology and Natural Resources of the Area Included by the Nipissing and Timiskaming Map-Sheets*. Report 962, Ottawa: Geological Survey of Canada, 1907.

Biggar, H.P., ed. *The Works of Samuel de Champlain*. 6 vols. Toronto: The Champlain Society, 1922.

Boudignon, Robert. Personal communications 1992–95. Historian, cottage owner in Delta.

Brillinger, Harold. Personal communications 1992–95. Marine Project Engineer at Public Works and Government Services Canada. Manager French River dams.

Brinkworth, Donna. *The Voyageur*. Manuscript in library at Old Fort William, Thunder Bay, 1982.

Brown, Craig, ed. *The Illustrated History of Canada*. Toronto: Lester & Orpen Dennys, 1987.

Brunton, Daniel F. *Life Science and Interpretive Potentials of the French River Study Area*. A Pilot Study for the Proposed Canadian Heritage Waterways System. Prepared for the Ontario Ministry of Natural Resources, Northeastern Region, Sudbury, November 1979.

Bullock, Peter. Personal communications 1992–95. Manager Environmental Services, City of North Bay.

Campbell, Marjorie Wilkins. *The Nor'Westers*. Toronto: Macmillan, 1958.

Campbell, William A. *Northeastern Georgian Bay and its People*. Britt: William Campbell, 1988.

———. *The French and Pickerell Rivers, Their History and Their People*. Britt: William Campbell, 1992.

Coopersmith, Penina. *Man-Made Heritage Component: Resource Identification and Evaluation*. Canadian Heritage Waterway System Pilot Study: The French River. Prepared for the Ministry of Natural Resources, Northeastern Region, Sudbury. Revised version, January 1980.

Cranston, J. Herbert. *Etienne Brûlé, Immortal Scoundrel*. Toronto: Ryerson Press, 1949.

Dictionary of Canadian Biography. Toronto: Univ. of Toronto Press.

Dokis, Leonard. Personal communications 1995. Band Elder Dokis First Nation. Owner–operator Riverview Cottages.

Fallis, Glenn. Personal communications 1990–95. Owner–operator Voyageur Canoes.

Francis, R. Douglas and Donald B. Smith., eds. *Readings in Canadian History, Pre-Confederation*. 4th ed. Toronto: Harcourt Brace, 1994.

Friends of French River Heritage Park. P.O. Box 142, Copper Cliff, Ontario, P0M 1N0.

Garvin, John W., ed. *Master-Works of Canadian Authors*. Vol. 3 of 25. Toronto: Radisson Society of Canada, 1927.

Gentilcore, R.L., and others. *Historical Atlas of Canada, Volume 2: The Land Transformed, 1800–1891*. Toronto: Univ. of Toronto Press, 1993.

Gibbon, John Murray. *The Romance of the Canadian Canoe*. Toronto: Ryerson Press, 1951.

Gilman, Carolyn. *Where Two Worlds Meet: The Great Lakes Fur Trade*. St. Paul: Minnesota Historical Society, 1982.

———. *The Grand Portage Story*. St. Paul: Minnesota Historical Society Press, 1992.

Gregg, John. Personal communications 1990–94. Owner Hunt Island in Upper French River.

Harris, R. Cole, and Geoffrey J. Matthews. *Historical Atlas of Canada, Volume 1: From the Beginning to 1800*. Toronto: Univ. of Toronto Press, 1987

Heidenreich, Conrad E. *Huronia: A History and Geography of the Huron Indians, 1600–1650*. Toronto: McClelland and Stewart, 1971.

Huang, John C. *Landscape Evaluation*. French River Canadian Heritage Waterway Pilot Study. Development Section, Parks and Recreational Areas Branch, Ontario Ministry of Natural Resources, March 1980.

Innis, Harold A. *The Fur Trade in Canada*. Toronto: Univ. of Toronto Press, revised edition 1970. First published 1930.

James F. Maclaren Ltd. *Report on a Flood Damage Reduction Study of the Sturgeon River / Lake Nipissing / French River System*. Report to Ontario Ministry of Natural Resources (three phases), 1980.

Kershaw, William. *Phase I: Preliminary Assessment of Recreation-Tourism and Other Land Uses*. French River Canadian Heritage Waterway Pilot Study, Ontario Ministry of Natural Resources, December 1979.

———. *Phase II: Summary of Resource Significance and Planning Issues*. Canadian Heritage Waterway System French River Pilot Study, Ontario Ministry of Natural Resources, March 1980.

———. *Draft Phase III: Directions for the Future*. The French River Canadian Heritage Waterway Pilot Study, Ontario Ministry of Natural Resources, April 1980.

Leatherdale, Murray. *Nipissing from Brule to Booth*. North Bay and District Chamber of Commerce, 1975.

Macdonald, Craig. Personal communications 1995. Outdoor Recreation Specialist, Ministry of Natural Resources, Algonquin Park.

Macfie, John. "Dredging Up the French's Past." In: Campbell, W. 1992.

Manual OFW. Interpretive manual in library at Old Fort William, Thunder Bay: no date.

Manual SMH. Interpretive manual in library at Ste. Marie Among the Hurons, Midland: 1992.

Maps
 French River Provincial Park map 1:50.000 (available from Ontario Ministry of Natural Resources, and Friends of French River Heritage Park).
 Topographical maps 1:50.000 and 1:250.000 (available from Ontario Ministry of Natural Resources).
 Ontario Base Maps 1:20.000 (available from Ontario Ministry of Natural Resources).
 Hydrographic Charts (available from Dept. of Fisheries and Oceans, Ottawa).

McClelland & Stewart. *Canadian Encyclopedia Plus, on CD-ROM*. Toronto: 1995.

Mckenzie, D. Ian. *Assessment of Earth Science Processes and Features of the French River, Ontario.* Prepared for the French River Canadian Heritage Waterway Pilot Study, Ontario Ministry of Natural Resources, December 1979.

Moroz, G.M. *The Effects of Water-Level Fluctuations on Recreation Values on the French River: a Summary.* Ontario Dept. of Lands and Forests, 1971.

Morse, Eric W. "Voyageurs' Highway." In *Canadian Geographical Journal,* May–July–August 1961. Reprinted in 1962 for the Quetico Foundation and the Minnesota Historical Society under the title: Canoe Routes of the Voyageurs.

———. *Fur Trade Canoe Routes / Then and Now.* Toronto: Univ. of Toronto Press, 1969. (Second edition 1979)

———. *Freshwater Saga.* Toronto: Univ. of Toronto Press, 1987.

Morse, Pamela. Personal communications 1995. Widow of Eric Morse.

Newman, Peter C. *Caesars of the Wilderness.* Vol. 2 of Company of Adventurers. Markham: Penguin Books, 1987.

Nute, Grace Lee. *The Voyageur.* St. Paul: Minnesota Historical Society Press, 1931; reprinted 1955.

———. *The Voyageur's Highway.* St. Paul: Minnesota Historical Society Press, 1941.

Ontario Ministry of Natural Resources. *French River Provincial Park Management Plan.* November 1993.

Pakkala, Helen, and Millie Hrnjez. *French River: Route to the Past.* Sudbury: The French River Heritage Foundation, 1979.

Palmer, Michael. Personal communications 1989–1995. Owner/operator Hartley Bay House and Marina.

Reid, Ron, and Janet Grand. *Canoeing Ontario's Rivers.* Vancouver: Douglas & McIntyre, 1985.

Roberts, Kenneth G. and Philip Shackleton. *The Canoe.* Toronto: Macmillan of Canada, 1983.

Rogers, Edward S. and Donald B. Smith, eds. *Aboriginal Ontario: Historical Perspectives on the First Nations.* Toronto: Dundurn Press, 1994.

Wheeler, Robert C. *A Toast to the Fur Trade.* St. Paul: Wheeler Productions, 1985.

———, and others. *Voices from the Rapids.* St. Paul: Minnesota Historical Society, 1975.

White, Randall. *Ontario 1610–1985.* Toronto: Dundurn Press, 1985.

Williams, Glyndwr. "The Hudson's Bay Company and The Fur Trade: 1670–1870." In *The Beaver,* Autumn 1983. Reprinted 1987 and 1991.

Wright, J.V. *Ontario Prehistory: An Eleven-Thousand-Year Archaeological Outline.* Ottawa: National Museum of Man, 1972.

Acknowledgments

The priceless help I have received in various ways from so many people and organizations during my work on this book is something I will always be grateful for. I am particularly indebted to Joseph Agnew, Shawn Allaire, Peter Ames, William Barrett, William Becket, Jocelyn Bertheaux, Tom Bell, Marc Bisaillon, Dave Bober, Robert Boudignon, Harold Brillinger, Beth and Dave Buckley, Peter Bullock, Jean Burgess, Rob Butler, Wayne Campbell, William Campbell, Canada's National History Society, Canadian Heritage Rivers Board, Canadian Recreational Canoeing Association, Canadian River Management Society, Trinela Cane and family, Canoe Ontario, Claude Chené, Eddie Chevrette, Mark Coté, Eric Crane, Richard Culpeper, Robert Desrochers, Leonard Dokis, Glenn Fallis, Ralph Frese, Friends of French River Heritage Park, Michael Greco, Jack Gregg, Michael Hall, Roger and Sandy Harris, Ria and Hassie Harting, Bob Henderson, Jim Hobbs, Bruce Hodgins, Don and Carolyn Hoshell, Judy Hulton, M.T. Kelly, Will Kershaw, Charles Laberge, Claude and Françoise Lacasse, Ron Lachance, Bill Lock, George Luste, Craig Macdonald, Oliver Macey, John Macfie, Hugh Macmillan, Melvin Mencher, Byron Moldofsky, Jean Morrison, George Moyal, Pamela Morse, Claire Muller, Bill Ness and family, Wally Nevin, Bob O'Hara, Ontario Arts Council, Ontario Recreational Canoeing Association, Michael Palmer and family, Sean Peake, David and Laurie Pelly, Herb Pohl, Jean Restoule, Bill Robinson, Royal Canadian Geographical Society, Pete Rysdale, Jim Sauve, Angus Scott, Dee Simpson, Gordon Simpson, John Simpson, Danny Smith, Harry Smith, Marvin Smith, Karl Stevens, Duncan Taylor, The Bennett Smith Heritage Foundation, Tony Urbanski, Charlotte and Harry Welch, Dean Wenborne, Wilderness Canoe Association.

Illustration Credits

Photographs: Toni Harting, except pages 8, 46, 78, 112, Pl. 16 by Ria Harting.

Current maps (Maps 1-20): Toni Harting and Roger Harris.

Aerial photographs (pages 90, 91): Ontario Ministry of Natural Resources. Used by permission.

Frances Anne Hopkins paintings (pages 99, 100, 106): National Archives of Canada: *Running a Rapid on the Mattawa,* C-13585; *Shooting the Rapids,* C-2774; *Canoe Manned by Voyageurs Passing a Waterfall,* C-2771; (page 110), Royal Ontario Museum: *Tracking the Rapids,* AC-952.168.2 (detail). Used by permission.

Paul Kane painting *French River Rapids* (page 109): Royal Ontario Museum: #912.1.2. Used by permission.

Historic maps, details (pages 94–97): National Archives of Canada: Champlain 1616, NMC-6333; Champlain 1632, NMC-51970; Coronelli 1688, NMC-6411; Bellin 1755, NMC-113509; Cary 1807, NMC-8515; Bouchette 1815, NMC-18392 1/2; Wyld 1843, NMC-15302. Geological Survey of Canada: Murray 1847-1857. Used by permission.

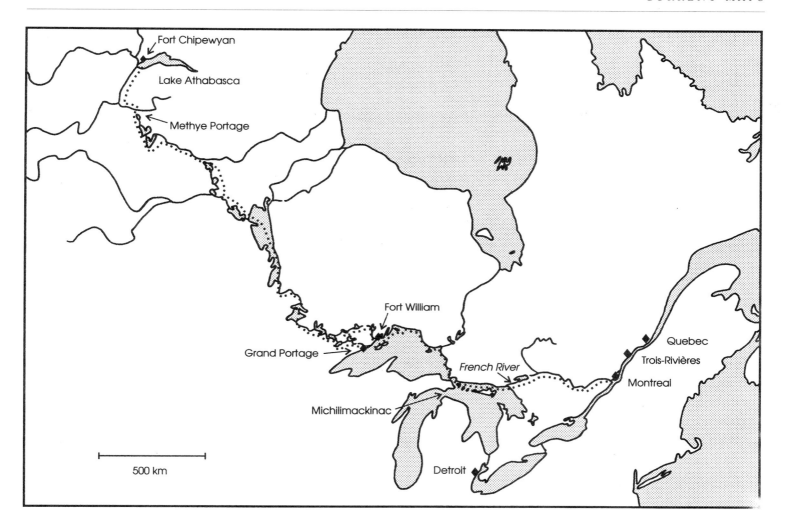

Fort Chipewyan

Lake Athabasca

Methye Portage

Fort William

Grand Portage

French River

Michilimackinac

Quebec

Trois-Rivières

Montreal

Detroit

500 km

MAP 1
*Main Fur-Trade Route of the
North West Company
1780s–1821*

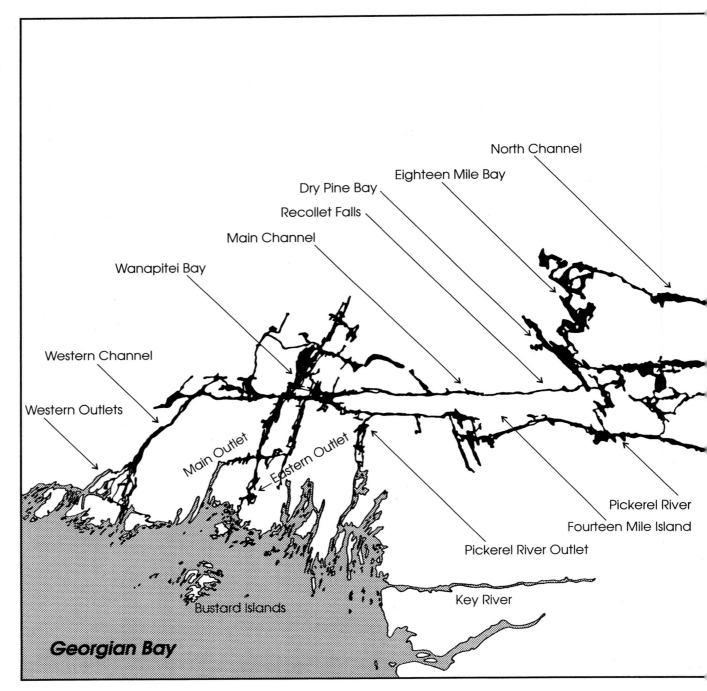

MAP 2
The French
River System

North Channel

Eighteen Mile Bay

Dry Pine Bay

Recollet Falls

Main Channel

Wanapitei Bay

Western Channel

Western Outlets

Main Outlet

Eastern Outlet

Pickerel River

Fourteen Mile Island

Pickerel River Outlet

Key River

Bustard Islands

Georgian Bay

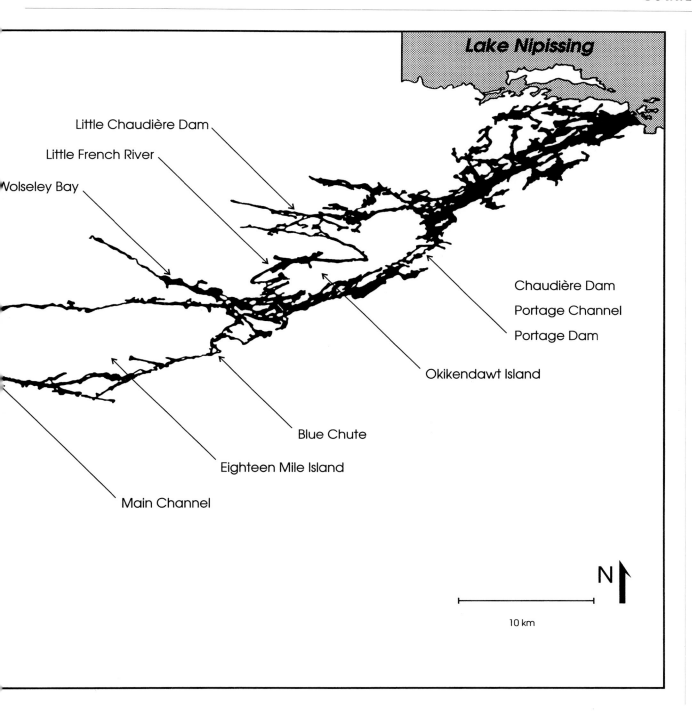

Lake Nipissing

Little Chaudière Dam

Little French River

Wolseley Bay

Chaudière Dam

Portage Channel

Portage Dam

Okikendawt Island

Blue Chute

Eighteen Mile Island

Main Channel

N

10 km

MAP 3
Major
Tributaries

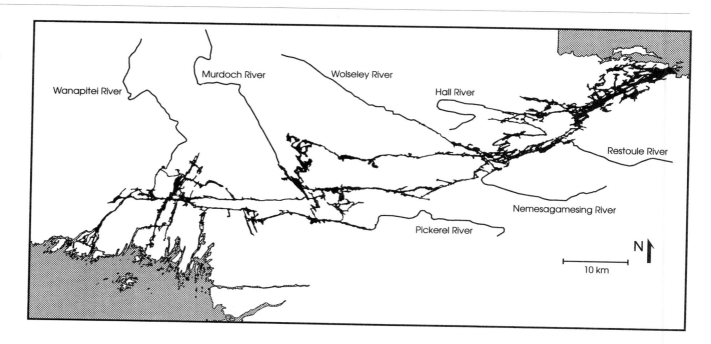

MAP 4
Highways -
Towns - First
Nations

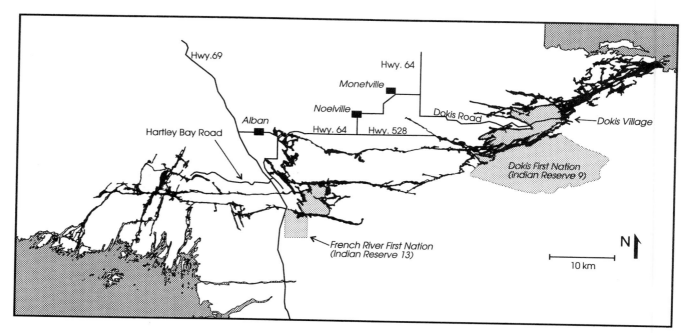

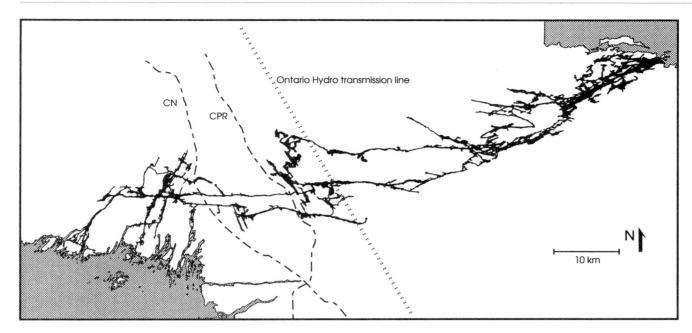

MAP 5
Railways -
Transmission
Line

Ontario Hydro transmission line

CN

CPR

N

10 km

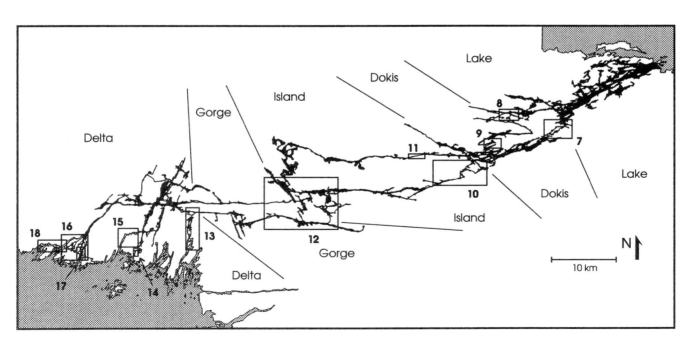

MAP 6
River
Sections -
Locations of
Detail Maps

Lake

Dokis

Island

Gorge

Delta

8

9

11

7

10

Lake

Dokis

Island

Gorge

Delta

18

16

15

13

12

17

14

N

10 km

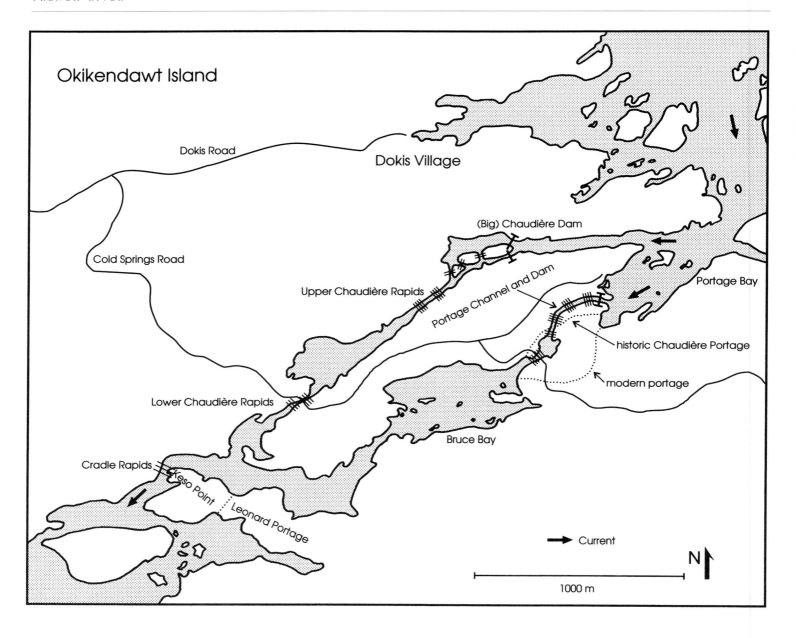

Okikendawt Island

Dokis Road

Dokis Village

Cold Springs Road

(Big) Chaudière Dam

Upper Chaudière Rapids

Portage Channel and Dam

historic Chaudière Portage

modern portage

Portage Bay

Lower Chaudière Rapids

Bruce Bay

Cradle Rapids

Keso Point

Leonard Portage

→ Current

N

1000 m

MAP 7
Chaudière Dam Area

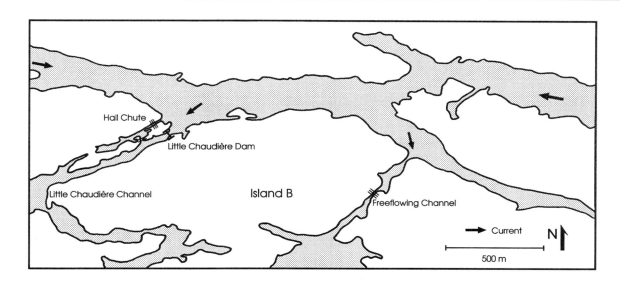

MAP 8
Origins of Little French River

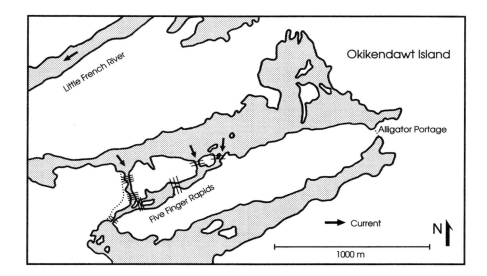

MAP 9
Five Finger Rapids Area

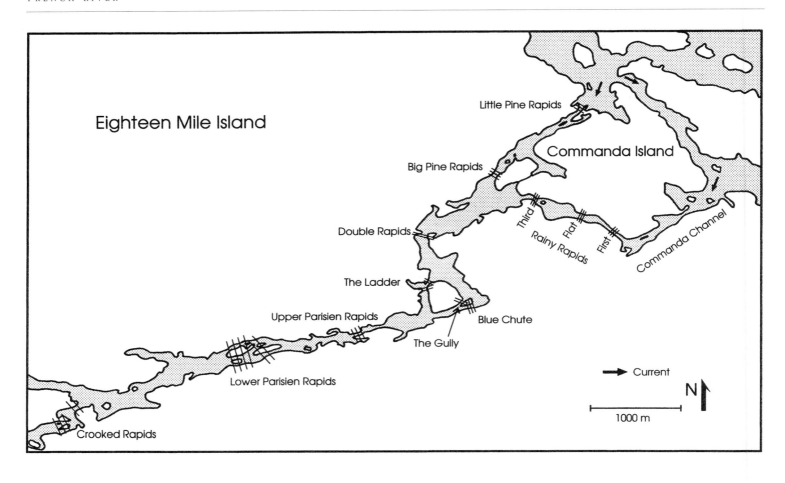

Eighteen Mile Island

Little Pine Rapids

Commanda Island

Big Pine Rapids

Double Rapids

Third

Flat

First

Rainy Rapids

Commanda Channel

The Ladder

Upper Parisien Rapids

Blue Chute

The Gully

Lower Parisien Rapids

Crooked Rapids

→ Current

N

1000 m

MAP 10
Five Mile Rapids

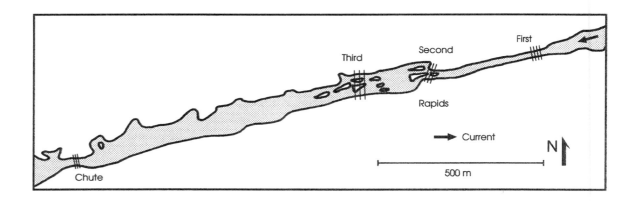

First

Second

Third

Rapids

Chute

→ Current

N

500 m

MAP 11
Cedar Rapids and Chute

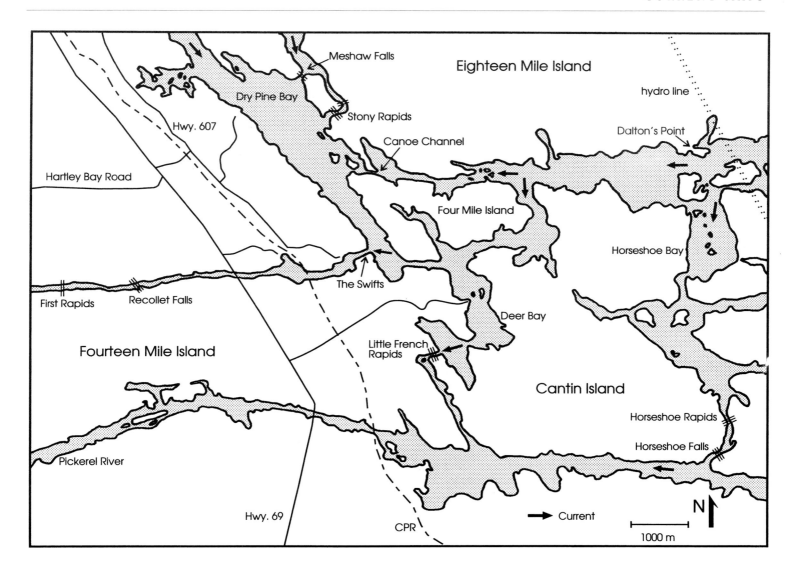

Meshaw Falls

Eighteen Mile Island

hydro line

Dry Pine Bay

Dalton's Point

Hwy. 607

Stony Rapids

Canoe Channel

Hartley Bay Road

Four Mile Island

Horseshoe Bay

The Swifts

First Rapids Recollet Falls

Deer Bay

Fourteen Mile Island

Little French
Rapids

Cantin Island

Pickerel River

Horseshoe Rapids

Horseshoe Falls

Hwy. 69

CPR

→ Current

N

1000 m

MAP 12
*Dry Pine Bay - Horseshoe Bay
Area*

LEFT, MAP 13
Pickerel River
Outlet

RIGHT, MAP 14
Eastern (Bass
Creek) Outlet

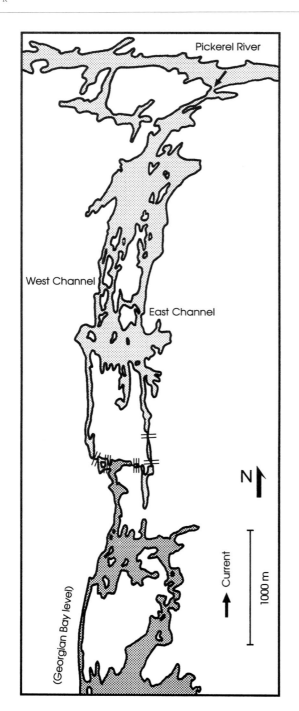

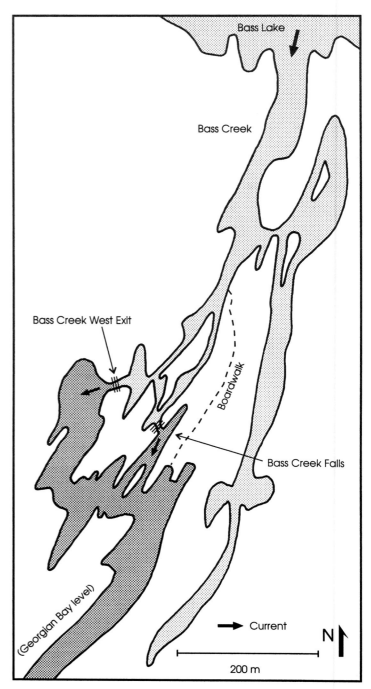

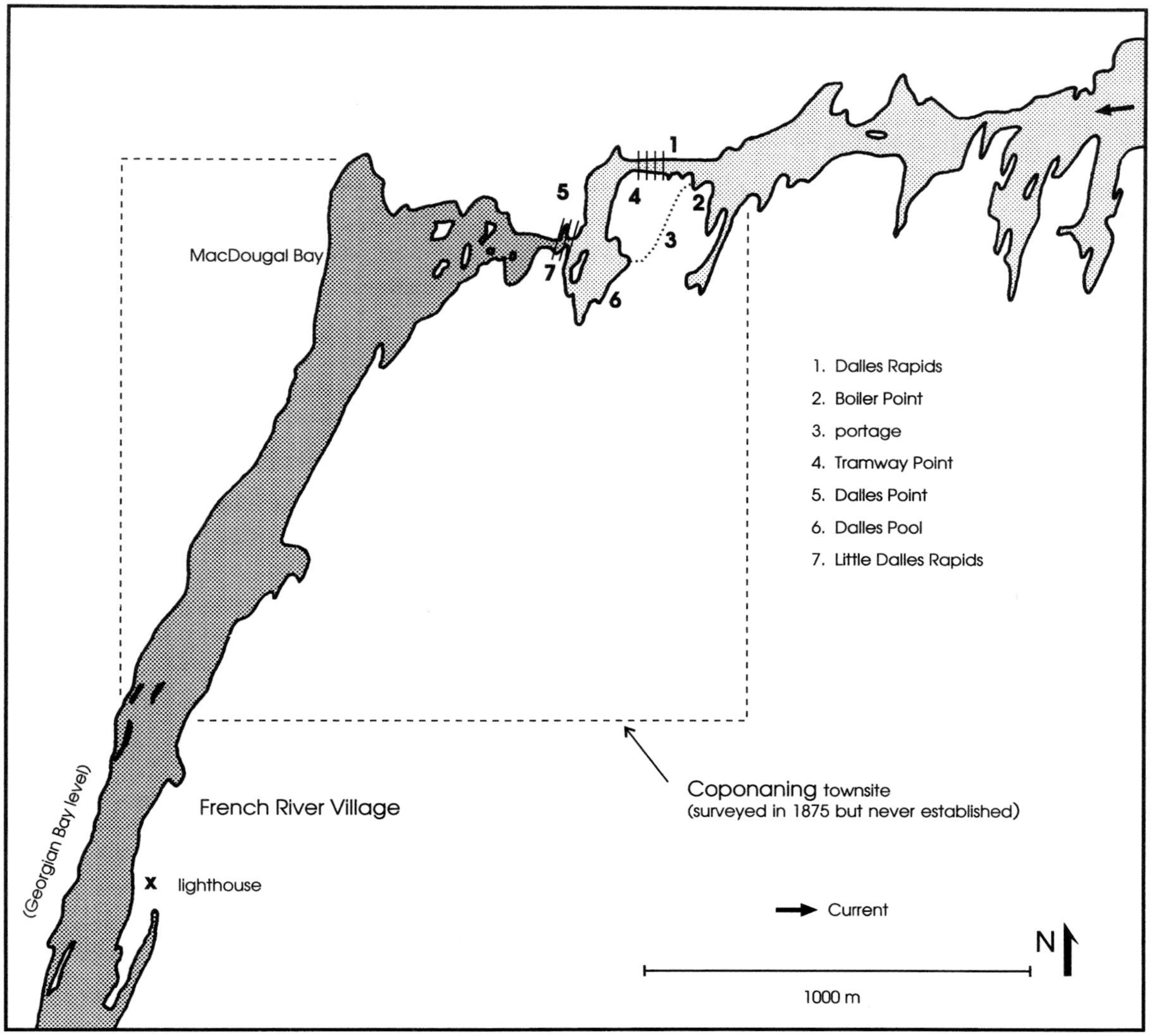
1
2
3
4
5
6
7
MacDougal Bay
1. Dalles Rapids
2. Boiler Point
3. portage
4. Tramway Point
5. Dalles Point
6. Dalles Pool
7. Little Dalles Rapids
Coponaning townsite
(surveyed in 1875 but never established)
French River Village
(Georgian Bay level)
x lighthouse
Current
N
1000 m

MAP 15
Main Outlet

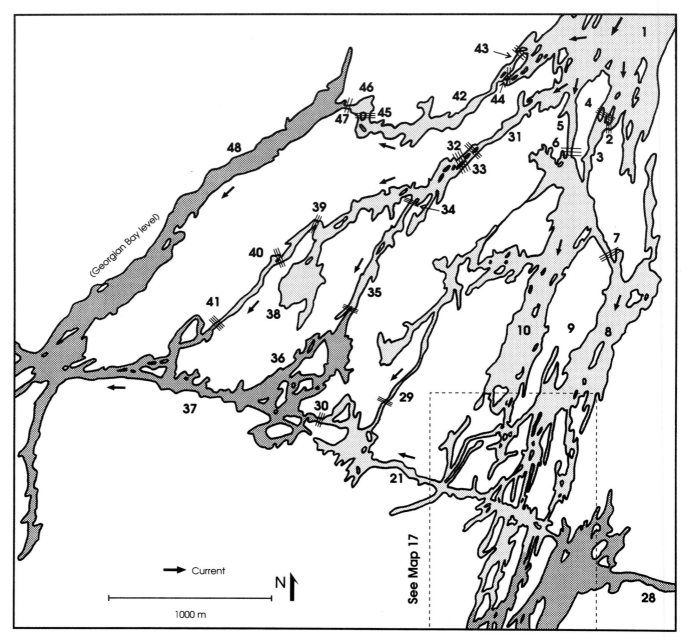

MAP 16
Western Outlets

Current

N

1000 m

(Georgian Bay level)

See Map 17

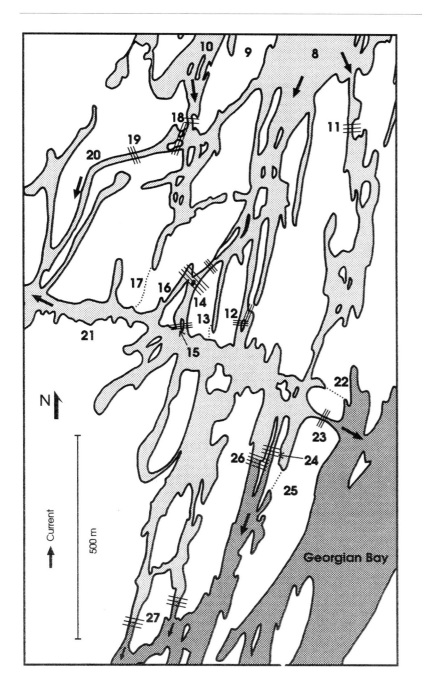

1. The Junction
2. Otter Rapids
3. Otter Channel
4. Middle Island
5. Boat Channel
6. First Swift
7. Second Swift
8. East Branch
9. Centre Island
10. West Branch
11. Herring Chute
12. Lily Chutes
13. Farley Portage
14. Crooked Rapids
15. The Jump
16. Back Channel
17. Hassie Portage
18. Lovers Rapids
19. Lovers Falls
20. Lovers Lane
21. High Cross Channel
22. Devil's Door Portage
23. Devil's Door
24. Little Jameson Rapids
25. Little Jameson Portage
26. Big Jameson Rapids
27. Harris Rapids
28. East Cross Channel
29. Herb's Channel and Falls
30. Cross Channel Rapids
31. Old Voyageur Channel
32. Rock Circus
33. East Channel
34. Boston Falls
35. Mills Channel
36. Shannon Bay
37. West Cross Channel
38. Morse Bay
39. Petite Faucille
40. Palmer Rocks
41. La Dalle
42. Voyageur Channel
43. Mushroom Channel
44. Marten Cut
45. Stamp Channel
46. Heron Bay
47. Washer Woman
48. Black Bay

MAP 17
Bad River Channel - High
Cross Channel

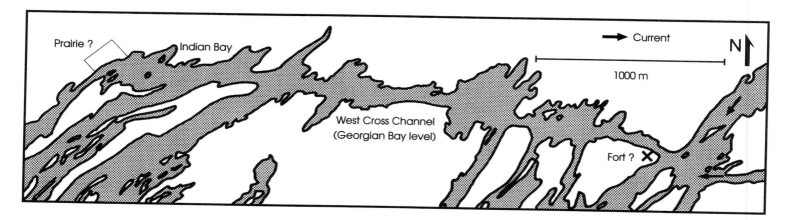

Prairie ?

Indian Bay

Current

N

1000 m

West Cross Channel
(Georgian Bay level)

Fort ? X

MAP 18
West Cross Channel

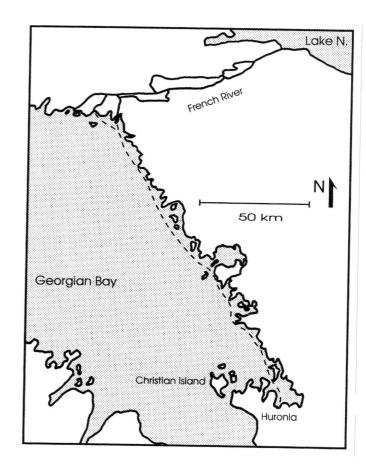

Lake N.

French River

N

50 km

Georgian Bay

MAP 19
Road to Huronia

Christian Island

Huronia

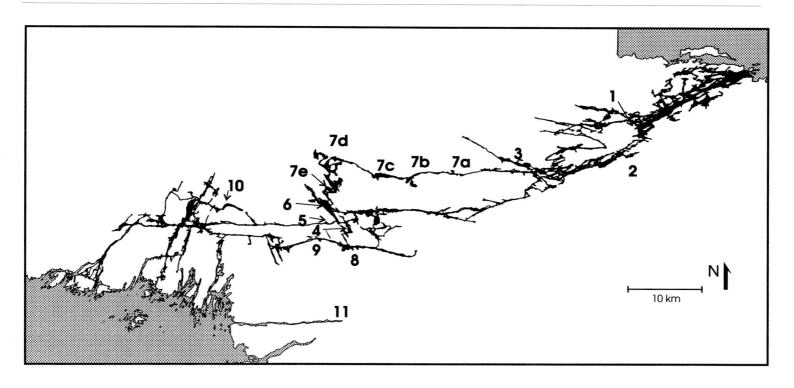

1. Dokis
   - 1.a Dokis Marina, (705) 763–2190
   - 1.b Migisi Marina, (705) 763–2114
   - 1.c Riverview Cottages, (705) 763–2127
   - 1.d Wajashk Cottages, (705) 763–2241
2. Cold Springs Cottages, (705) 763–2362
3. Wolseley Bay
   - 3.a public dock
   - 3.b Totem Point Lodge, (705) 898–2562
   - 3.c Waverly Lodge, (705) 898–2381
   - 3.d Pine Cove Lodge, (705) 898–2500
4. Deer Bay Park, (705) 857–2543
5. Main Channel
   - 5.a Schell's Camp and Park, (705) 857–2031
   - 5.b French River Supply Post, (705) 857–2128
6. Loon's Landing, (705) 857–2175
7. North Channel
   - 7.a Ash Bay public access
   - 7.b Rainbow Camp and Trailer Park, (705) 898–2356
   - 7.c Green Bay Lodge and Trailer Park, (705) 898–2747
   - 7.d Presqu'ile Camp, (705) 857–2195
   - 7.e Martin's Camp and Trailer Park, (705) 857–5477
8. Trottier Store and Trailer Park, (705) 857–2536
9. Pickerel River
   - 9.a public dock
   - 9.b Smith Marine, (705) 857–2722
   - 9.c Pickerel River Marina, (705) 857–2522
10. Hartley Bay House and Marina, (705) 857–2073
11. Frenette's Key Marina Resort, (705) 383–2308

MAP 20
Some Road Access Points

For those coming north via Highway 69, these are a few of the places where canoes can be rented: Algonquin Canoe and Kayak Store, Waubaushene, (705) 538–0881; White Squall, Noble, (705) 342–5324 (sea kayaks); Frenette's Key Marina, Key River, (705) 383–2308; Grundy Lake Supply Post, Highway 522, (705) 383–2251. A few canoe rental locations are also available south of Sudbury on Highway 69.

INDEX